The Gettysburg Campaign

*A Captivating Guide to the Military
Invasion of Pennsylvania That Culminated
in the Battle of Gettysburg During the
American Civil War*

Free Bonus from Captivating History
(Available for a Limited time)

Hi History Lovers!

Now you have a chance to join our exclusive history list so you can get your first history ebook for free as well as discounts and a potential to get more history books for free! Simply visit the link below to join.

Captivatinghistory.com/ebook

Also, make sure to follow us on Facebook, Twitter and Youtube by searching for Captivating History.

Table of Contents

Introduction

Almost 160 years after the conclusion of the American Civil War, the conflict and its ramifications continue to preoccupy national interest. The bloodiest of all American wars, the four years of battle from 1861 to 1865 killed an estimated 650,000 to 850,000. Many of the simmering controversies that erupted into outright war had been present since the founding of the United States.

Abolitionists pointed to the amoral practice of African slavery, especially as it pertained to America's expansion into the western territories and matters of representation and taxation. Rather than deal with the hot-button issue, the delegates to the Constitutional Convention had settled on the Three-fifths Compromise in 1787, which allowed three out of five slaves to be counted as a person in determining a state's population. In side-stepping the problem, the founders all but guaranteed future conflicts over slavery that predictably erupted as the nation spread westward.

The economic roots of the war lay in an unbalanced burden of tariffs between the agricultural South and increasingly industrial North. This imbalance proved telling when the North successfully blockaded Southern ports, effectively denying the Confederacy the manufactured goods it could only obtain as imports.

Finally, during the Reconstruction years, adherents of the "Lost Cause" staunchly defended the war as a matter of constitutional interpretation. These apologists sought to mythologize and justify the Southern position, as evidenced by the persistence of the phrase "War of Northern Aggression" in reference to the conflict. Even now, in the 21st century, opponents of a strong central government rail against federal overreach and speak of states' rights and secession.

In 1861, the motivations that led men to fight on either side ranged from a reckless desire for adventure to passionate advocacy for a given political position. Most did not understand, however, that advances in weaponry were quickly ending the days of gentlemanly warfare and chivalrous cavalry charges. For the first time in the 1860s, massed troops armed with weapons and ammunition produced by the Industrial Revolution faced one another in bloody, bludgeoning battles with staggering casualties numbering in the hundreds of thousands. The 1863 Gettysburg Campaign, culminating in the three-day battle of Gettysburg (July 1-3, 1863) surpassed them all.

No one can say for certain how the rank and file gathered in the fields of Pennsylvania felt about facing one another in battle so close to the eighty-seventh anniversary of the Declaration of Independence. Many of the accounts penned by veterans in the following years were colored by fading or convenient memories. Contemporaneous letters reflected fear, hunger, hope, and weariness.

In his epic 1974 fictional account of the Gettysburg campaign, *The Killer Angels: A Novel of the Civil War*, Michael Shaara attempted to capture the gravitas inherent in the pedigrees of some of the combatants. Crafting a scene that involved Confederate General Lewis Armistead and a British observer, Shaara had Armistead recite the Revolutionary War heritage of soldiers within his line of sight.

That conversation never happened, but the grandsons of distinguished patriots were there on those three hot days in July 1863— on both sides of the confrontation. Robert E. Lee himself was the son of "Light Horse" Harry Lee, who served as one of George Washington's officers.

Union Colonel Paul J. Revere, grandson of the eponymous patriot, suffered shrapnel to the throat on the second day at Gettysburg and died forty-eight hours later. Armistead, who died after being wounded in Pickett's Charge, was the nephew of Major George Armistead, who defended Ft. McHenry in the War of 1812 with such gallantry Francis Scott Key was moved to write "The Star-Spangled Banner."

President John Tyler's grandson, Private Robert Tyler Jones, fought for the Confederacy, as did the commander of the 53rd Virginia

Infantry, Colonel William Aylett, the grandson of Patrick Henry. General Alexander Webb, who commanded the Union Philadelphia Brigade, was the grandson of a minuteman who fought at Lexington in 1775.

Undoubtedly, countless others could trace their lineage to predecessors who were instrumental in founding the United States of America, if not by acts worthy of the history books, then certainly by the sweat of their brows.

Lee's Decision to Invade Pennsylvania

After racking up a string of victories in Virginia, Confederate General Robert E. Lee decided to take the fight to the North in the summer of 1863. He counted on growing anti-war sentiment on the northern home front to force the Union to negotiate a peace. Instead, Lee suffered a crippling defeat at Gettysburg that signaled the beginning of the end for the Southern cause.

The Confederacy would hold on until Lee's surrender at Appomattox Courthouse on April 9, 1865—approximately twenty-one months after the pivotal battle. Lee, however, never again went on the offensive after his ill-fated excursion into Pennsylvania. Going into the Gettysburg Campaign, the general believed the fight inside Union territory would determine the outcome of the war; he was right, but not in the way he anticipated.

Eight decades of simmering regional disputes preceded the Gettysburg campaign. The immediate precipitator of Lee's decision to move into Pennsylvania, however, lay in his victory over Maj. Gen. Joseph Hooker at Chancellorsville, a clash regarded as Lee's "perfect" battle. Waged in Virginia from April 30 to May 6, 1863, Chancellorsville set in motion the chain of events that led to Gettysburg. Buoyed by the victory, the Southern commander turned the 75,000 men of the Army of Northern Virginia northward into enemy territory.

Lee hoped to put enough pressure on Washington, D.C., to compel peace negotiations, but his strategy was also driven by the hunger of his men and their ragtag condition. Virginia's resources were spent. The North offered abundant crops and manufactured goods. The invasion meant the Confederates could eat off the land, confiscating food and badly needed supplies.

Hooker followed Lee as he moved north, but kept his distance, unwilling to see a repeat of Chancellorsville. Hooker's caution frustrated

President Abraham Lincoln, who knew that support for the war in the North was at an all-time low. In June, Lincoln replaced Hooker with Maj. Gen. George Gordon Meade, whose orders were to use the 90,000 men in the Army of the Potomac to prevent Lee from reaching Washington, D.C.

Three corps of Southern troops crossed the Potomac on June 15, 1863. By the 28th, they were on the banks of the Susquehanna River in Pennsylvania. Unfortunately, Lee's movements were hampered by a lack of on-the-ground intelligence from General Jeb Stuart's cavalry. Lee's decision to converge his forces on Gettysburg was thus made more on instinct than hard tactical data.

The area's major roads converged in Gettysburg, and Lee wanted control of those roads—a desire that committed 165,620 soldiers to participate in the largest battle ever to take place on American soil. Of those men, 93,921 were Union troops, and 71,699 were Confederate. All were Americans.

Chapter 1 – June 1863

After the Confederate victory at Chancellorsville in May 1863, the Army of Northern Virginia and the Army of the Potomac faced one another on either side of the Rappahannock River near Fredericksburg, Virginia. Though a Southern victory, Chancellorsville did not tip the scales of war definitively, resulting in a stalemate on the same ground the armies had held for five months. Ironically, the combatants were positioned almost equidistant from their capitals—Washington lay fifty-three miles to the north and Richmond fifty-seven miles south.

Any dissection of the Gettysburg campaign must begin with some attempt to understand General Robert E. Lee as both a commander and Southern figurehead.

Robert E. Lee

The son of Revolutionary War hero Henry "Light Horse Harry" Lee III, Robert Edward Lee spent the first thirty-two years of his career as an engineer with an excellent reputation. A graduate of the United States Military Academy at West Point, Lee served as the school's superintendent following his distinguished service in the Mexican-American War. His wife, Mary Anna Custis Lee, was George Washington's great-granddaughter.

Much has been made of Lee's anguish over the broken Union and his pained decision to resign his commission and join the Confederate Army after Virginia seceded in 1861. The fact that he did so, however, undeniably made him a traitor to the nation he had served so honorably.

Though a philosophical opponent of slavery (because he believed the institution harmed the white owners), Lee's conscience did not prevent him from listing several hundred human beings as his property. He admitted to the belief that enslaved African were his racial inferiors and that they did, in some ways, benefit from their forced servitude. In his eyes, slavery compelled blacks to develop a work ethic and introduced them to Christianity.

After serving as a military adviser to Confederate President Jefferson Davis in 1861, Lee assumed command of the Army of Northern Virginia in June 1862. He drove the Federal (Union) forces away from Richmond, the Confederate capital, and scored a victory at the Second Battle of Bull Run in August.

In September, Lee invaded Maryland only to retreat to Virginia after the Battle of Antietam, which showed no gains for either side. His subsequent victories in the summer of 1863 at Fredericksburg and Chancellorsville proved critical to his second invasion of the north, the Gettysburg Campaign.

Opinions of Lee's skill as a general range from the open worship of his soldiers and the hagiography of biographers to the critical evaluations of military historians. In retrospect, many of his decisions—including that to remain and fight for a third day at Gettysburg—appear to be sheer folly. Lee did not write a memoir to clarify his decisions, and his official dispatches were too impersonal to offer insights for posterity.

Most modern interpretations agree that although Lee provided a focal point of inspiration for his troops, he did not manage the Battle of Gettysburg well. Though there were moments throughout the war when Lee appeared to read the minds of his opponents—most of whom he knew personally—he was not a good communicator with his subordinates. That failure surfaced more than once at Gettysburg.

There are facts and suppositions about Lee during the Gettysburg campaign that are worthy of consideration. At age 56, he battled both heart trouble and rheumatism. Some scholars contend he suffered from dysentery. He was undoubtedly exhausted and arguably over-confident. At battle's end, however, Lee looked for no excuses to explain away his defeat. He assumed full responsibility for the debacle in Pennsylvania.

After the battle, Lee stayed on the defensive for the remainder of the war. He never mounted another head-on assault as he'd done with Pickett's Charge on July 3, 1863. In the end, Grant simply trapped Lee, forcing the general into a long series of retreats against superior forces, culminating in the Confederate surrender at Appomattox Courthouse on April 9, 1865. Lee refused all entreaties to continue the fight with guerilla forces, considering such a desperate move an ungentlemanly denial of defeat.

Many people continue to regard Lee as the Confederacy's finest general—perhaps one of the nation's greatest military minds—but that iconic status stems more from the personal respect Lee commanded than his tactical brilliance. By the standards of his day (his stance on slavery notwithstanding), Lee appears to have been an honorable man called to a dishonorable cause. He most certainly is a study in contrast.

After the war, Lee lost the right to vote, and his family home was confiscated to become Arlington National Cemetery. He was not, however, arrested or punished in any other way. Over time, Lee evolved into a symbol of national reconciliation, even visiting Ulysses S. Grant at the White House in 1869.

Yet Lee opposed giving the vote to formerly enslaved Africans. Though asked to condemn the Ku Klux Klan, he remained silent on that organization's violent tactics and on white supremacy in general. Critics argue that a public stance by Lee could have eased the worst excesses of the Reconstruction and post-Reconstruction eras, but that seems to accord almost super-human power to his influence.

As a civilian, Lee served as the president of Washington College from 1865 until his death in 1870 at age 63 following a stroke. The school is now Washington and Lee University, where Lee is buried.

Lee's Second Invasion

Lee's decision to invade the North for a second time represented what would become the most ambitious Southern offensive of the war. All other considerations aside, the campaign was, at its heart, a mass supply raid. War-ravaged Virginia was depleted of the needed resources to feed and equip an army, while the rich Northern farms were ripe for the taking.

By abandoning his defensive positions along the Rappahannock, Lee would upset the Union's planned summer campaigns by threatening the major cities of Philadelphia, Baltimore, and Washington, D.C. As mentioned, he hoped to capitalize on what he perceived to be growing anti-war sentiment in the North, an understanding gained primarily from reading Peace Democrat or "Copperhead" newspapers.

Those materials did not, however, give Lee an appreciation for President Abraham Lincoln's determination to win the war or for the effect of Major General Ulysses S. Grant's western campaigns on Northern morale. From May 1-17, Grant scored victories at Port Gibson, Raymond, Jackson, Champion Hill, and the Big Black River Bridge before cornering 30,000 Confederates under Lt. Gen. John C. Pemberton at Vicksburg. When a relief force commanded by General Joseph E. Johnson failed to rescue their Confederate compatriots, Grant settled in to wait out the siege.

Jefferson Davis called Lee to Richmond twice in May 1863 to discuss strategy. Given the location of the Federal troops, the two leaders had good reason to fear for the safety of the Southern capital. Additionally, the Confederate hold on the entire Tidewater region was called into serious question by a Union garrison of 20,000 troops in Suffolk that threatened Norfolk and Hampton roads.

With Vicksburg under siege and Virginia on tenuous ground, Davis had no single, comprehensive solution at his disposal. As his understanding of the situation evolved, he wanted Lee to take at least 20,000 men and go to Pemberton's relief at Vicksburg, but the general's thoughts were elsewhere.

In February, Lee had secretly asked Lt. Gen. Thomas J. "Stonewall" Jackson's chief engineer to craft a map of the valley of Virginia that would extend as far as Philadelphia. By April, Lee told Confederate Secretary of War James A. Seldon he was contemplating crossing into Maryland in May.

Despite all objections, Lee's position won out in the strategic talks. He insisted victory lay in concentrating his movements in the Northeast. The planned invasion reflected almost to the letter the general's execution of the Maryland Campaign in 1862.

Beyond his misreading of the Northern home front, Lee also placed an excessive degree of faith in the fighting spirit of his men after Chancellorsville. In his correspondence, Lee fantasized about his tested veterans creating a general panic in Pennsylvania, leading to the utter destruction of the Army of the Potomac. While ready for battle, Lee's men were hardly as "invincible" as their commander believed them to be.

Still, Davis approved the northern offensive, with Lee issuing his first orders ahead of the invasion on June 3. The Army of Northern Virginia moved away from Fredericksburg to concentrate around Culpepper. Though they marched with all stealth, Union General Joseph Hooker, in command of the Army of the Potomac, learned of their movements on June 5.

Joseph Hooker

Hooker, a native of Hadley, Massachusetts (born 1814), graduated twenty-ninth of fifty in the West Point Class of 1837. Known as a hard drinker with an eye for the ladies, Hooker served in the Seminole Wars and the Mexican-American War as a staff officer for Winfield Scott and future president Zachary Taylor.

He resigned his commission in 1853 after being involved in a controversy that put him at odds with General Scott. Hooker testified against Scott during a court-martial regarding insubordination—an act of disloyalty that Scott apparently did not forget or forgive.

As a civilian, Hooker was both bored and unsuccessful, failing as a farmer, land developer, and politician but standing out as a gambler and womanizer. By 1858, he wanted back in the army and wrote to the Secretary of War seeking a commission as a lieutenant colonel.

When nothing came of the request, he found a place with the California militia as a colonel. At the outbreak of the Civil War, Hooker again requested a commission but was rejected, likely because Scott was general-in-chief of the army.

Ultimately, Hooker appealed to Lincoln directly, gaining an appointment as a brigadier general of volunteers, organizing and training elements of the Army of the Potomac near Washington, D.C., under Maj. Gen. George B. McClellan.

During the 1862 Peninsula Campaign, Hooker earned a battlefield reputation for aggressive but exemplary action at Williamsburg and Seven Pines. Though his headquarters was always the scene of revelry, even in the heat of war, Hooker was known for putting the welfare of his men above all else, with special sensitivity for their morale.

After his promotion to major general in July 1862 and following the Second Battle of Bull Run, Hooker was given command of the troops that became the Army of the Potomac's I Corps. He led his men at South Mountain and Antietam, where they fought Confederate Lt. Gen. Stonewall Jackson's forces to a standstill. Hooker, however, was forced to retire from the confrontation due to an injured foot. Afterward, he maintained the battle would have been a resounding Union victory had he remained on the field.

In September 1863, Hooker was promoted to brigadier general in the regular army. Throughout this period, he criticized the actions of his superiors, finding McClellan too slow and cautious and McClellan's replacement, Maj. Gen. Ambrose Burnside, a poor strategist. Some of Hooker's complaints trod the fine line of insubordination. Burnside even drafted a letter to Lincoln insisting Hooker was unfit for service in the current national crisis.

Fortunately for Hooker, however, Lincoln's patience with his generals had grown thin. The president fired Burnside and put Hooker at the head of the Army of the Potomac on January 26, 1863. The president counted on "Fighting Joe" Hooker's aggressive reputation to gain positive traction for the Union forces. The new commander started by improving the quality of his camp's food, sanitation, health care, and providing more generous furloughs for the men.

In other areas of innovation, Hooker established the army's first intelligence organization, the Bureau of Military Information, and approved a system of corps badges. The emblems were meant to create a sense of pride and ease unit identification during the chaos of battle. Officer training became more organized, and cavalry units were integrated into a designated corps.

Despite the effectiveness of these moves and the changes he made in command personnel, Hooker's personal conduct failed to meet the standard of his rank. One junior officer described the general's headquarters as little better than a brothel. Hooker surrounded himself with loyal cronies that added a layer of politics to his command, and he continued to drink.

Hooker planned an ambitious summer campaign that would result in the capture of Richmond. Instead, he suffered an embarrassing defeat at Chancellorsville, where proximity to a cannonball strike left him with a concussion. Refusing to relinquish command, Hooker made decisions that other officers found questionable in the aftermath of the fighting.

When Lee unexpectedly moved north, Hooker's mission was to protect Washington, D.C., at all costs before finding and defeating the Southerners. Yet again, Lincoln was losing confidence in his commander and would soon welcome the opportunity to replace him just as he'd ousted McClellan and Burnside.

Brandy Station

On June 5, when Hooker learned of Lee's movements, he dispatched Maj. Gen. Alfred Pleasonton with 4,000 infantry and artillery and 7,000 cavalrymen to pursue the Confederates. Pleasonton surprised Confederate Maj. Gen. Jeb Stuart at Brandy Station in the early morning hours of June 9.

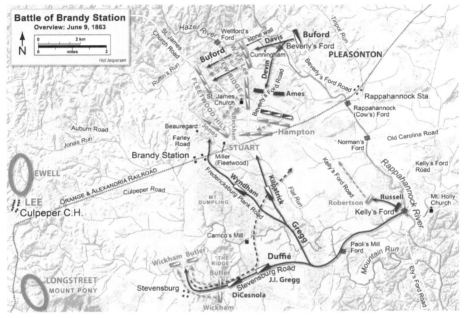

Map of the Battle of Brandy Station.
Map by Hal Jespersen, www.cwmaps.com, CC BY 3.0
<https://creativecommons.org/licenses/by/3.0>, via Wikimedia Commons;
https://commons.wikimedia.org/wiki/File:Brandy_Station_Overview.png

The fighting there evolved into one of the largest mounted confrontations of the war. Stuart commanded five cavalry brigades, approximately 9,500 men, under Brigadier Generals Wade Hampton, W.H.F. "Rooney" Lee, Beverly H. Robertson, William E. "Grumble" Jones, and Colonel Thomas T. Munford (in temporary command of Brig. Gen. Fitzhugh Lee's troops).

The flamboyant Stuart was almost captured but rallied to hold his ground. At the end of the day, the Union forces suffered 907 casualties to the Confederate's 523. In the fighting, Lee's son, Rooney, was seriously injured and captured later that month. While Stuart styled the confrontation as a victory, the Southern newspapers were less complimentary. Neither the close call in which his best cavalry general was surprised nor negative public opinion deterred Lee, however, in the execution of his ambitious plans for invasion.

James Ewell Brown "Jeb" Stuart

Jeb Stuart's name figures heavily among the officers whose conduct at Gettysburg received heavy post-war criticism. Stuart was a native Virginian born in 1833. Stuart's father was a War of 1812 veteran and a politician, serving in both houses of the Virginia General Assembly and the U.S. House of Representatives. His grandfather fought in the American Revolution.

Educated at home until age twelve, Stuart enrolled in Emory and Henry College at 15. He tried to enlist in the army for the first time in 1848 but was rejected due to his youth. In 1850, however, he received an appointment to West Point, where he prospered. When Robert E. Lee became the academy's superintendent in 1852, Stuart quickly became a friend of the family.

Stuart graduated 13th in a class of forty-six in 1854 and was dispatched to far West Texas, where he served at Fort Davis with the U.S. Regiment of Mounted Riflemen. He transferred to the cavalry in 1855 and was sent to Kansas. He saw action against various Native American tribes and during the outbreak of violence that preceded the Civil War, known as "Bleeding Kansas."

Stuart resigned his commission on May 3, 1861, and joined the Confederate Army as a lieutenant colonel with the Virginia Infantry. On July 4, Stuart assumed command of all cavalry companies in the Army of the Shenandoah under Thomas J. "Stonewall" Jackson. This consolidation led to the formation of the 1st Virginia Cavalry Regiment. By 1862, he held the rank of brigadier general and, a few months later, major general.

Known for his plumed hat and flowing cloak, Stuart performed admirably in all the major campaigns leading up to Gettysburg. There, however, his lack of contact with the main body of Lee's army for more than a week led to a rare rebuke from his commander and lingering post-war criticism. Like General James Longstreet, Stuart became a scapegoat for the Confederate defeat. Detractors insist that had Stuart kept Lee informed of Union troop movements, the battle would have resulted in a decisive victory.

Though not disciplined for his absence, Stuart was not promoted to lieutenant general when given a corps command in 1863. Unlike other Gettysburg general officers who lived to defend themselves, Stuart was struck down at the Battle of Yellow Tavern on May 11, 1864, dying the next day at only 31. A bullet had pierced Stuart's left side, and the projectile went through his stomach, missing the spine by only an inch. Taken to Richmond by ambulance, Stuart was coherent, ordering that his son receive his sword and spurs. The general received a visit from President Davis but died at 7:38 p.m. on May 12. His widow, Flora, wore black for the remainder of her life, passing in 1923. Known as one of the greatest cavalrymen in American history, Stuart received a sort of posthumous knighthood in the eyes of the very Southerners who had denounced his actions at Gettysburg.

Hooker's Resignation

In the wake of Brandy Station, Lee continued preparations to move north with his reconfigured army, changes put in place after the death of Stonewall Jackson on May 10. Adding a third corps to the Army of Northern Virginia, Lee would now rely on Lt. Gen. James Longstreet in command of the I Corps, Lt. Gen. Richard S. Ewell of the II Corps, and Lt. Gen. Ambrose Powell Hill of the III Corps. With the addition of Stuart's cavalry, Lee's combined strength was 75,000 men.

After concentrating at Culpepper, Lee planned to drive the Federals out of the Shenandoah Valley before moving north into the Cumberland Valley of Pennsylvania. By keeping the Blue Ridge Mountains to his right (east), Lee could shield his supply trains and those he intended to send south with confiscated goods.

On June 10, Lee directed Ewell to move into the Shenandoah Valley as the lead element of the invasion. The II Corps was home to most of Stonewall Jackson's troops, who had marched into the same region during the 1862 Valley Campaign.

After the Union defeat at Brandy Station, Hooker clearly understood that Lee was on the march north. In response, he wanted to move on Richmond, only to face a sharp rebuke from Lincoln, who reminded him that the objective was Lee's army, not the southern capital. Consequently, Hooker pursued of Lee on June 13 with 94,000 men comprised of seven infantries and one cavalry corps. Regardless of the numbers, however, Hooker believed that Lee (who had 75,000 men) outnumbered him.

The Union general's pessimism was fueled by the loss of thousands of veterans whose two-year enlistments had just ended. He was also nagged by the fact that some of his corps contained only two rather than three divisions. Hooker expressed his doubts by bombarding his higher-ups for reinforcements or permission to take control of units not currently under his command.

As Ewell moved north, he encountered Union Brig. Gen. Robert H. Milroy's garrison at Winchester on June 14. The Southerners assailed the position and scattered the Federals, capturing 4,000 prisoners, 300 wagons of supplies, and 23 cannons. Following a scouting mission by cavalry under the command of Brig. Gen. Albert G. Jenkins, Ewell's infantry marched into Pennsylvania on June 20.

Over the next week, Ewell's men made themselves at home in the south-central portions of the state. Raiding parties reached the vicinity of the state capital at Harrisburg. On June 21, Lee issued General Orders 72, in which the procedures for foraging were laid out. The officers in charge of supplies—quartermaster, commissary, ordnance, and medical—were directed to pay fair market prices for the goods they required. Soldiers were directed to exercise proper respect for private property.

Predictably, however, these directives were violated, leading Lee to issue a follow-up order scolding his men and reminding them of the conduct expected of them by the rules of civility and Christianity. Regardless, heavily laden wagons began to roll South, some carrying African Americans arrested regardless of their status as free or slave.

Many Pennsylvania residents snatched up all they could carry and ran from the Confederates. The chaotic response from the government and from troops whose protection the civilians should have rightly expected only worsened their distress. Neither the Lincoln administration's June 9 creation of the Department of the Susquehanna nor calls from Governor Andrew G. Curtain resulted in any substantive moves toward local defense.

When the 26th Pennsylvania Emergency Regiment attempted to confront Ewell's troops on June 26, they panicked after the first shots were fired. Those who weren't captured turned tail and ran. Moving toward Harrisburg, Ewell dealt with only sporadic and ineffective resistance.

Lee's troops, however, faced a different set of circumstances. Hooker, now aware of his adversary's presence, looked for a way to intercept the

Confederates through gaps in the Blue Ridge. On June 17 at Aldie, June 19 at Middleburg, and June 21 at Upperville, Jeb Stuart's cavalry clashed with mounted Federal units. Lee specifically ordered Stuart to engage in actions intended to harass and delay Hooker, especially if the Federal troops attempted to cross the Potomac.

If the Federal troops did get across the river, Stuart was to assume a position to the right of Lee's column as it continued north. In following his orders, Stuart was certainly an annoyance to the Federals and a worry to Washington. In picking his route, however, Stuart put Hooker between his own troops and Lee's for a week at the end of the month. This critical error deprived Lee of the high-quality intelligence necessary to plan his actions as circumstances increasingly put Gettysburg in the crosshairs of both armies.

Persistent in his belief that Lee outnumbered him, Hooker continued his calls for reinforcements, finally saying that if he did not receive additional troops, he would resign. Lincoln and Secretary of War Edwin M. Stanton called the general's bluff and accepted his resignation. Maj. Gen. George G. Meade was appointed to replace Hooker on June 28.

In his haste to leave the area, Hooker failed to give Meade a detailed assessment of the situation in Pennsylvania. Thus, Meade took command of the Army of the Potomac with scant knowledge of the forces he led and even less understanding of the enemy he faced. Making only essential changes regarding organization and administration, Meade immediately sent out multiple requests for information and tried to formulate a plan.

George Gordon Meade

Meade, born December 31, 1815, in Spain, grew up in Philadelphia, where he attended a private military school until his father's death in 1828. On July 1, 1831, Meade, who wanted to become a lawyer, entered West Point. He took little pleasure in his time there, though he graduated 19th in the Class of 1835.

After fulfilling his required year of army service, Meade resigned and sought employment with his brother-in-law in Florida as a railroad surveyor. He did similar work on the Texas-Louisiana border and the border between Maine and Canada. All these jobs had been in connection with the Army Corps of Topographical Engineers, which could no longer hire civilians after 1842.

Subsequently, Meade rejoined the army as a second lieutenant to continue his career. He saw battlefield service in the Mexican-American War and then assisted in putting down the Seminole tribe in Florida. In the early 1850s, Meade oversaw the construction of a lighthouse in the state before being assigned to survey Lake Huron and Lake Michigan.

At the outbreak of the Civil War, Meade was appointed a brigadier general of volunteers and given command of the 2nd Brigade of the Pennsylvania Reserves, assigned to construct defenses in Washington, D.C. When the Army of the Potomac was divided into four corps in March 1862, Meade served under Maj. Gen. Irvin McDowell in the I Corps.

After being wounded at Glendale in June 1862, he recuperated in Philadelphia, resuming command at the Second Battle of Bull Run. His men participated in the battles of South Mountain and Antietam. Meade assumed temporary command at the latter when Hooker, the corps commander, was wounded. In September 1862, after John Reynolds took command of the I Corp, Meade was placed in command of the Third Division.

The decision to place Reynolds over the I Corps left Meade, who had more combat experience, greatly frustrated. His feelings were somewhat improved with a promotion to major general in November ahead of the Battle of Fredericksburg, where Meade's men broke the Confederate lines even though his attack received no reinforcement. Meade led the V Corps at Chancellorsville, but his troops were held in reserve during the fighting, contributing to the Union defeat.

On the morning of June 28, Meade learned that he had been appointed to replace Hooker. He was not the president's first choice; John Reynolds turned down the job. In the end, however, Gettysburg proved to be a decisive victory for the North and led to Meade's promotion as a brigadier general in the regular army.

Meade retained command of the Army of the Potomac after Lt. Gen. Ulysses S. Grant was given command of all Union armies in March 1864. After the Battle of Spotsylvania Court House, Meade was promoted to major general. In the closing months of the war, Meade felt slighted on multiple occasions when less experienced generals received greater favor. Though present during the Appomattox Campaign, Meade was not on site for Lee's surrender. The Army of the Potomac disbanded on June 28, 1865.

Many of Meade's issues with his fellow generals lay in his political position. He opposed slavery only as the issue that caused the Union to be severed, not as a moral matter. To him, the war's only goal was preserving the United States, not freeing enslaved people.

Meade possessed a notoriously short temper and, though respected, was not an inspirational leader. Nicknamed "Old Snapping Turtle," Meade could be social and courteous when not under stress but abrasive and combative in the thick of war. He tended toward recklessness and paranoia.

After the war, as commander of the Department of the South, Meade oversaw the re-entry of Alabama, Florida, Georgia, North Carolina, and South Carolina into the Union. He died in Philadelphia in 1872.

Find and Fight the Enemy

On June 29, Meade ordered the Army of the Potomac to continue moving north, even though the general didn't know his opponent's location or goals for the next twenty-four hours. As a result, Meade opted to concentrate his troops on Pipe Creek in Maryland, south of the Pennsylvania border. Though this move was subsequently criticized as a reluctance to face Lee, Meade was fully prepared to take the offensive once he better understood the situation at hand.

Lee learned of Meade's appointment on June 29. He assumed Meade would initially be cautious in a new command but still ordered the Army of Northern Virginia to converge at Cashtown, seven miles northwest of Gettysburg. Lee instructed his corps commanders not to engage with Meade's forces until the entire Army of Northern Virginia was present. By the next day, the Southern III Corps had arrived in Cashtown. Longstreet was still west of the Blue Ridge, and Ewell was preparing to de-camp at Carlisle and march on July 1.

Chapter 2 – Tuesday, June 30, 1863

On Tuesday, June 30, 1863, Union Brigadier General John Buford, in command of the 1st Division of the Army of the Potomac, rode into Gettysburg. From a distance, Confederate soldiers under the command of General J. Johnston Pettigrew spotted Buford's troops.

Because of this chance encounter, Pettigrew and Buford came to separate but equally fateful conclusions. Pettigrew was convinced there was a significant Federal presence near Gettysburg but proved incapable of persuading his superiors of that fact. Buford recognized the importance of controlling the roadways that converged in Gettysburg and denying the Confederates access to the high ground south of town. Though uncertain of Lee's exact location, Buford knew the enemy he'd glimpsed west of town would be back in greater numbers.

Thanks to his decision to stay the night and hold his position with only two small brigades—approximately 2,800 men—and a battery of six guns, Buford chose the ground upon which the Battle of Gettysburg was fought.

John Buford, Jr.

Buford, a West Point graduate, was born to a slave-holding father in Woodford County, Kentucky, on March 4, 1826. He spent his boyhood in Rock Island, Illinois. After one year at Knox College, he was accepted into the West Point Class of 1848.

During his time at West Point, Buford's upperclassmen included future Southern generals Stonewall Jackson and George Pickett—the man destined to lead a fatal charge against the Union center on the third day of the Battle of Gettysburg.

Serving in Texas, Kansas, and Utah, Buford remained loyal to the Union and declined a commission in the Confederate Army. Like many Civil War commanders, however, his career and heritage provided striking twists in Buford's wartime experiences. His grandfather, Simeon Buford, served under Henry "Lighthorse" Lee during the American Revolution.

In 1854, Buford married Martha McDowell Duke, known as Pattie to her friends. They had two children, a son and a daughter. The bulk of Pattie's people sided with the South.

Buford distinguished himself at the Second Battle of Bull Run in August 1862, Antietam in September of the same year, and Stoneman's Raid in the spring of 1863. He was 37 in July 1863 and had only five months to live, succumbing to complications of typhoid in December 1863.

On the day of Buford's death, Lincoln promoted him to major general for his distinguished service at Gettysburg. Ironically, one of the people with the general when he died was his African-American servant, Edward.

Lincoln attended the funeral in Washington, D.C. Buford was buried at West Point next to another hero of Gettysburg, Lieutenant Alonzo Cushing, who died defending Cemetery Ridge, the very "high ground" that first attracted Buford's attention on June 30.

J. Johnston Pettigrew

A native of North Carolina, James Johnston Pettigrew was born on July 4, 1828. He studied law, taught at the United States Naval Observatory, and wrote a book about Spanish culture all before the age of 30.

When the Civil War broke out, he joined Wade Hampton's Legion as a private but soon accepted a colonel's commission with the 1st South Carolina Rifle Militia Regiment. By the summer of 1862, President Davis promoted Pettigrew to brigadier general.

At the Battle of Seven Pines in May and June 1962, Pettigrew nearly bled to death from a m wound to the throat and shoulder. He was also shot in the arm and suffered a bayonet wound to the leg. Though left for dead, he awakened a prisoner of war. Two months later, he was part of a prisoner exchange and returned to service.

At Gettysburg, Pettigrew commanded a brigade of 2,500 men in the Army of Northern Virginia as part of Major General Henry Heth's division in Lieutenant General A.P. Hill's Third Corps. On July 1, 1863, after Heth was wounded, Pettigrew assumed command of the division. During the retreat, Pettigrew's brigade served as the army's rear-guard unit. On the morning of July 14, they were among the last Confederate troops still in Union territory on the north side of the Potomac. While positioning his men on the front line, Pettigrew took a bullet to the abdomen fired by a cavalryman in the nearby Michigan Brigade. Refusing to be left behind and captured, Pettigrew was taken over the river. He died at Edgewood Manor plantation on July 17. The general was buried in North Carolina, where a day of mourning was observed in his honor.

Tuesday, June 30, 1863

Buford, at the head of two brigades of cavalry—approximately 3,000 men—rode into Gettysburg early on the morning of June 30. The locals greeted him joyously, relieved to see Union soldiers in the town's streets after having played brief host to Confederate General Jubal Early four days earlier. (Early's men marched out of Gettysburg on June 27.)

During his short occupation, Early had demanded the town fathers produce salt, flour, sugar, coffee, onions, bacon, and whiskey, along with a thousand pairs of shoes, 400 hats, and $5,000. The town council president, David Kendlehart, refused but told Early that Gettysburg's shops would be open for trade.

To the ragtag Southerners, Gettysburg looked like a prosperous town, but the lack of food was real and worsened thanks to their presence and the coming days of battle. With the destruction of the Rock Creek railroad bridge leading to Gettysburg, the populace would be cut off from its usual supply lines. As happy as they would be to see Lee's men retreat on July 4, they were happier still to see wagons arrive with badly needed provisions. One woman recalled grabbing an orange and eating every bite, including the seeds.

Still, the people of Gettysburg distributed food and drink to Buford's exhausted, hungry troopers. Local girls burst into patriotic songs to offer encouragement to the men. Young boys visited Buford's camp and offered to ride the horses to water. Anxious to keep his men in fighting form, Buford had the local newspaper print placards forbidding the sale or gifting of liquor to his men.

In addition to the demand for supplies, Early's presence had also struck terror among Gettysburg's African-American residents, who fled, rightfully fearing they would be rounded up and sent south. Most went east, with some sheltering near Culp's Hill. As recorded by Mary Elizabeth Montford, a woman known as Aunt Beckie declared she was going into the hills rather than be returned to slavery. A man called "Bow-Legged Jack" hid under a haystack for four days without food rather than face the Southerners.

It's unclear exactly how many material goods the Confederates confiscated in Gettysburg, although general ransacking certainly occurred. One thing they did not receive, however, was information from the populace. When questioned about the location of Union troops, the citizens professed to know nothing. Thus, their show of elation when Buford arrived was quite real.

A.P. Hill's Movements

As Buford arrived in Gettysburg, Confederate General A.P. Hill was forced to position his troops without the advantage of reports from advanced cavalry scouts. By then, General Jeb Stuart and his mounted troops had been out of touch with the main body of Lee's army for almost a week.

Instead, Hill sent Pettigrew toward Gettysburg on the Chambersburg Pike with about 2,700 infantrymen from North Carolina. Pettigrew had orders not to engage should he meet the enemy.

Dr. John William Crapster O'Neal

Along the way, the Confederates stopped and questioned Dr. John William Crapster O'Neal, who insisted there were no Union soldiers in Gettysburg. Rather than risk setting loose a spy, O'Neal was detained.

When Pettigrew spotted mounted Union cavalry on a ridgeline outside Gettysburg (John Buford's men), the doctor was forced to defend himself. O'Neal swore those Union soldiers had not been there when he left town to make a call on the Chambersburg Pike. He was telling the truth because he'd narrowly missed the arrival of Buford's men.

During the battle, O'Neal tended soldiers from both armies. He was largely responsible for recording Confederate gravesites in the aftermath, including names and regimental data when available. The doctor published this information in 1866, leading various southern groups to raise sufficient funds to repatriate large numbers of their war dead.

Pettigrew Backs Off

Regardless of when the Federals arrived in Gettysburg, Pettigrew saw them and obeyed his orders. He withdrew to Marsh Creek, where he met generals Hill and Henry Heth. The most recent intelligence indicated the Union Army was still in Maryland, leaving Hill to conclude Pettigrew had seen only scouts. Heth agreed but asked if he might take his division back to Gettysburg the next day. Hill gave his permission.

The decision to return to the town made Pettigrew uneasy, however. He was sure he'd seen Union cavalry in Gettysburg (and he had). Additionally, the Union infantry camp lay perilously close—only six miles away at Emmitsburg, Maryland, making rapid reinforcement in the face of an engagement a dangerous possibility.

Chapter 3 – Wednesday, July 1, 1863

At sunrise on July 1, a day that would prove to be hot and humid, Heth marched east from Cashtown on the Chambersburg Pike. There is a myth that he and his men wanted to confiscate shoes from a factory in Gettysburg, but no such enterprise existed in the town.

In arranging his marching column, Heth made the unconventional decision to lead with Major William J. Pegram's artillery battalion, followed by infantry under Brig. Gens. James J. Archer and Joseph R. Davis. In total, almost 14,000 Confederates set to march down Chambersburg Pike at 7 a.m.

Around 7:30 a.m., they encountered light resistance approximately three miles west of Gettysburg before engaging more aggressively with Union Colonel William Gamble's dismounted cavalry troopers. Credit for the first shot of the battle goes to Marcellus Jones, a lieutenant in the Eighth Illinois Cavalry.

The Federals, armed with breech-loading carbines, laid down rapid fire from behind fence posts and similar cover. The weapons allowed the Union soldiers to fire two to three times faster than men armed with muzzle-loaded rifles. Additionally, there was no need to stand to reload, which allowed the Federal troops to remain behind cover. Both factors created the false impression that a much larger force stood between the Confederates and Gettysburg.

Although Lee had ordered Hill not to engage the enemy until the entire Army of Northern Virginia was present, Heth had a fight on his hands. He outnumbered Buford's dismounted cavalry, but the Federals were deployed with the high ground at their backs—principally Oak Ridge, McPherson's Ridge, and Seminary Ridge.

Buford had chosen his positions well to execute a delaying action against superior forces. His men repeatedly stood their ground until the last possible second before imminent capture, then retreated and made a new stand—all in the name of buying time for Major General John F. Reynolds with the XI Corps to arrive, trailed by Major General Oliver O. Howard. Once on the field, Buford intended to assume even stronger defensive positions south of town on Cemetery Hill, Cemetery Ridge, and Culp's Hill.

Given the situation, Heth deployed his brigades rather than wait for the rest of the division. By about 10:20 a.m., the Southerners had reached Herr Ridge and pressed the Federals east to McPherson Ridge.

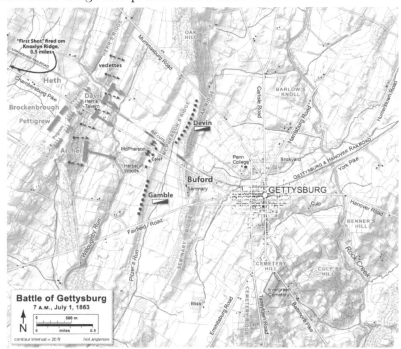

Map of the Battle of Gettysburg's actions on the first day.
This file is licensed under the Creative Commons Attribution 3.0 Unported license. Attribution: Map by Hal Jespersen, www.posix.com/CW; https://commons.wikimedia.org/wiki/File:Gettysburg_Day1_0700.png

John F. Reynolds

John Fulton Reynolds, a career army officer, would die later that day at only forty-two. A native of Pennsylvania born September 21, 1820, in Lancaster, he graduated in the West Point Class of 184; he and saw duty in Florida, South Carolina, and Texas. He was promoted to the rank of major in the Mexican-American War. During the conflict, he formed close friendships with Winfield Scott Hancock and Lewis A. Armistead.

From September 1860 to June 1861, Reynolds served as the Commandant of Cadets at West Point, where he taught tactics. At the outbreak of the Civil War, he declined a position as aide-de-camp to Lt. Gen. Winfield Scott, instead accepting an appointment as a lieutenant colonel in the 14th U.S. Infantry. Soon after, he was promoted to brigadier general and sent to Washington, D.C., but was diverted for service with the Army of the Potomac under Maj. Gen. George B. McClellan.

After participation in the Peninsula Campaign in 1862, Reynolds's brigade suffered a brutal Confederate attack at the Battle of Beaver Dam Creek on June 26-27. Reynolds was captured when he fell asleep after two days with no rest. He was sent to Libby Prison in Richmond only to be freed in a prisoner exchange on August 15.

On the second day of the Second Battle of Bull Run, Reynolds led a charge that stopped the Confederate advance and bought the Union Army time to execute an orderly retreat. Promoted to the rank of major general on November 29, 1862, after the Battle of Fredericksburg, he clashed with Hooker over the order to retreat at Chancellorsville.

President Lincoln met with Reynolds on June 2, 1863, to ask if he would assume command of the Army of the Potomac. Lincoln could not meet Reynold's request to act free of political restraint, however, and the post went to Meade on June 28.

At Gettysburg, Reynolds occupied the town on July 1, establishing defensive lines to the north and west. But, as he was supervising the placement of troops at Herbst Woods, a bullet struck, killing him instantly. The Union Army keenly felt the loss of the man widely considered the North's best general. Reynolds's actions on July 1 committed the outnumbered Army of the Potomac to the fight. He was buried in Lancaster, Pennsylvania, on July 4, 1863. Three statues at the Gettysburg National Military Park commemorate his participation in the battle.

Reynolds Arrives

The infantry exchanges during the morning of July 1 happened on the north and south sides of the Chambersburg Pike, with most of the fighting along McPherson Ridge. In this area, the Confederate brigade under General Joseph R. Davis fought the Federals under Brig. Gen. Lysander Cutler, with three Union regiments on the north side of the pike and two on the south.

Immediately to Cutler's left, the Federal Iron Brigade (1st Brigade, 1st Division, I Corps) under Brig. Gen. Solomon Meredith fought Confederate General James J. Archer's troops. Reynolds was responsible for positioning both Cutler and Meredith's brigades.

Most accounts place Reynolds on the battlefield by mid-morning. His arrival marked the end of the first of four phases of fighting on July 1 to the west of Gettysburg. From 7 a.m. until roughly 10:15, the fighting was relatively light and all under the command of officers with no greater seniority than division commander. The second phase began with the arrival of Reynolds and lasted until noon, with two brigade-level infantry actions to either side of the Chambersburg Pike on McPherson's Ridge.

Reynolds immediately met with Buford and then began deploying his infantry units. The timing of what happened next is up for considerable debate. After getting Cutler and Meredith in place and bringing up Captain James A. Hall's Maine battery, Reynolds was on horseback at the east end of Herbst Woods between 10:15 and 10:30 a.m.

The general was positioning the 2nd Wisconsin Infantry Regiment when he stood in the saddle to examine the terrain. Some witnesses said he was looking through a pair of field glasses. A musket ball struck Reynolds in the back of the neck, passing through his head and exiting the eye socket. (Other accounts say the shot struck him behind the ear.)

Reynolds fell forward, while his terrified horse galloped toward the open fields, only to be captured by the general's aides. A detail of men from the 76th New York carried the body, wrapped in an army blanket, to the nearby Lutheran Seminary. The source of the fatal shot remains in dispute, variously attributed to a sniper, random, and even friendly fire.

Reynolds was the highest-ranking officer of either army to die at Gettysburg. After the war, multiple Confederate veterans claimed to have killed Reynolds, but none of the accounts or alternative theories associated with his death have ever been conclusively verified.

With Reynold's death, command passed to Major General Abner Doubleday. The North had lost not only an inspirational leader but also a general with the acumen to effectively manage the unfolding battle. Although Reynolds's troop placements set the subsequent course of the day's battle, he was not there to oversee the outcome.

Doubleday in Command

As the fighting raged on after Reynold's death, Davis's Confederate brigade laid down fire on three of Cutler's Union regiments. Before the Federals could get in position, the Southern troops overlapped their line. The Federals fell back to Seminary Ridge. In what amounted to half an hour of fighting, Cutler's forces suffered a 45 percent casualty rate.

Meanwhile, Archer's Confederates faced heavy resistance from the Union Iron Brigade. When the Confederates reached the far side of Willoughby Run and began the climb into Herbst Woods, the longer Union line enveloped their position on the right.

During the fighting, Private Patrick Molony of the 2nd Wisconsin captured Archer when he discovered the general taking cover in a thicket. Archer was a slight man with a frail constitution but a tenacious disposition. He resisted, but Molony prevailed. Thus, Archer became the first of Lee's general officers to be taken prisoner. When escorted behind enemy lines, he encountered Doubleday, whom he knew from the regular army, and the two men exchanged greetings.

Imprisoned at Johnson's Island on the Lake Erie Coast, Archer suffered greatly from exposure to the poor weather. After a year, he was transferred to Fort Delaware, where he became one of the 600 officers shipped to Morris Island, South Carolina, to act as hostages to stop the constant Confederate shelling.

Exchanged in 1864, Archer rejoined the Confederate army, serving at the Siege of Petersburg before his health failed him completely. He died on October 26, 1864, at age 46.

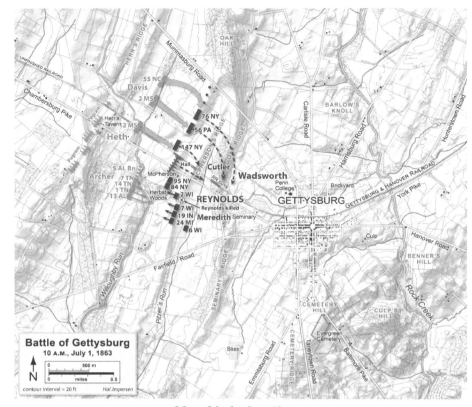

Map of the battle at 10 a.m.

Abner Doubleday

A career army officer, Abner Doubleday, fired the first shot of the Civil War in defense of Fort Sumter on April 12, 1861. His grandfathers served in the Revolutionary War, his mother's father riding as a messenger for George Washington at only fourteen.

Doubleday graduated 24th of fifty-six cadets in the West Point Class of 1842. He served in the Mexican-American War and the Seminole Wars and, as a captain, was second in command at Ft. Sumter under Major Robert Anderson. For the remainder of his life, Doubleday would refer to himself as the "hero" of Sumter.

An artilleryman by training, Doubleday commanded both the Artillery Department in the Shenandoah Valley in 1861 and Maj. Gen. Nathaniel Bank's artillery in the Army of the Potomac during the

Peninsula Campaign. Known as a commander ready to seize the initiative for his actions at Brawner's Farm before the Second Battle of Bull Run, Doubleday fought gallantly at Antietam, where he was wounded by shrapnel from an exploding shell.

For his bravery at Antietam, Doubleday received the brevet rank of lieutenant colonel in the regular army and then major general of volunteers. His division remained mostly idle at the Battle of Fredericksburg and was held in reserve at Chancellorsville.

Doubleday's battlefield decisions at Gettysburg are considered his finest of the war. After John Reynold's death, Doubleday held off ten Confederate brigades for five hours. On July 2, however, Meade replaced Doubleday with Maj. Gen. John Newton based largely on the incorrect assertion by XI Corps commander Maj. Gen. Oliver O. Howard that Doubleday's corps had broken and caused the collapse of the Union line. In truth, Meade and Doubleday had long been at odds. Though he fought honorably for the remainder of the battle, Doubleday never forgot Meade's snub.

Sustaining a wound to the neck on July 2, Doubleday received a brevet promotion to the rank of colonel, but Meade refused to reinstate his corps command. Returning to Washington on July 7, Doubleday served out the war performing administrative duties in charge of court-martials with only one brief return to combat.

While in Washington, Doubleday testified against Meade to the Congressional Joint Committee on the Conduct of War. There, Doubleday harshly criticized Meade's actions at Gettysburg. A loyal Lincoln man, Doubleday rode with the president to Pennsylvania for the delivery of the Gettysburg Address on November 19, 1863.

After the war, as a colonel in the regular army, Doubleday served in San Francisco and Texas, where he commanded an African-American regiment stationed at Fort McKavett. Following retirement in 1873, Doubleday wrote two books about the Civil War, practiced law, and became an active member of the Theosophical Society. He died in January 1863 and is buried in Arlington National Cemetery.

In the end, Doubleday's greatest fame lies in the claim that he invented the game of baseball, but considerable evidence disputes this.

The Railroad Cut

With Davis's Southerners in disarray, Doubleday moved the 6th Wisconsin toward them around 11 a.m. Pausing at the fence running along the Chambersburg Pike, the Federals stalled Davis as he attacked Cutler's position. Joining the 84th and 95th New York, the three Union regiments charged the railroad cut where the Confederates had taken cover.

At the time, however, Davis was nowhere to be found. He had left his men in an untenable position in the cut, which was fifteen feet deep in places, preventing effective fire. Still, the Southerners fought tenaciously. As the Union continued to advance, hand-to-hand fighting broke out, with bayonets drawn. The bloodshed continued until Major John Blair, in command of the 2nd Mississippi, surrendered to Colonel Rufus Dawes of the 6th Wisconsin.

Confusion reigned on that section of the battlefield, where the Confederates could not engage in substantive fighting for the remainder of the day. Of the 1,707 Southern troops committed to that area, 500 were killed or wounded, with more than 200 taken prisoner.

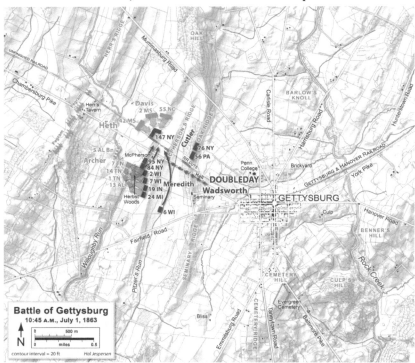

Map of the battle at 10:45 a.m.

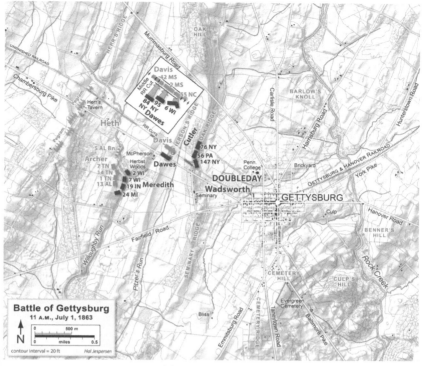

Fighting at the railroad.

The Field at Midday

By 11:30 a.m., Confederate General Henry Heth, who had been
ered by Lee not to engage, had not only done so but appeared to be
the losing side of the ensuing battle. Southern reinforcements arrived
12:30 p.m., however, under the command of General Pettigrew,
onel John M. Brockenbrough, and Major General Dorsey Pender.
litionally, Ewell was marching on Gettysburg from the north, and
al Early's four brigades were moving toward the town along the
risburg Road.

Doubleday used the brief lull to reorganize the Union lines,
ngthening both ends with newly arrived troops commanded by
adier General Thomas A. Rowley. It was not until 11:30 that Major
eral Oliver O. Howard learned of Reynold's death, which placed
in command of the Union troops. Calling for reinforcements from
III and XII Corps, Howard shored up his positions, placing two

artillery batteries on Cemetery Hill, which was designated as a Federal rallying point should other positions fall.

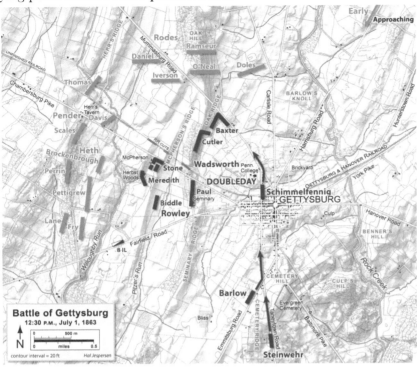

Position of forces at 12:30.

This file is licensed under the Creative Commons Attribution 3.0 Unported license. Attribution: Map by Hal Jespersen, www.posix.com/CW; https://en.wikipedia.org/wiki/File:Gettysburg_Day1_1230.png

The third phase of the day's fighting opened at approximately 2 p.m. By that time, both sides benefited from the arrival of considerable reinforcements. The fighting that had begun west of town now extended to the north side, and General Lee had arrived to take tactical control of the Southern positions.

Ewell's Southerners were on the field and confronting Union troops positioned on Oak Hill. Seeing the Union placement as preparatory to an attack, Ewell set aside Lee's order regarding a general engagement—a somewhat moot point, as the battle had begun at 7 o'clock that morning.

The Confederates under Major General Robert E. Rodes attacked with three brigades (Doles, O'Neal, and Iverson), facing elements of the Union I and XI Corps. Iverson and O'Neal's men fared poorly against x regiments under Union Brigadier General Henry Baxter.

Performing no reconnaissance, Iverson sent his men against Federal oops positioned behind a stone wall. The Federals waited until the onfederates were within a hundred yards to lay down withering fire that opped the Confederates in almost perfect lines. The area of the ttlefield, now known as Iverson's Pits, is regarded as one of the most unted places at Gettysburg.

By 3 p.m., Baxter's exhausted Federals were replaced by Gabriel R. ul's brigade, facing Confederate Brigadier Generals Junius Daniel and odson Ramseur. Paul held against Ramseur's initial attack but took a llet through the temples that left him permanently blind. He did, wever, survive to live another twenty years.

Daniel moved to the southwest to break the Federal I Corps line only see the fighting devolve into a stalemate against the 149th nnsylvania, known as the "Bucktail Brigade."

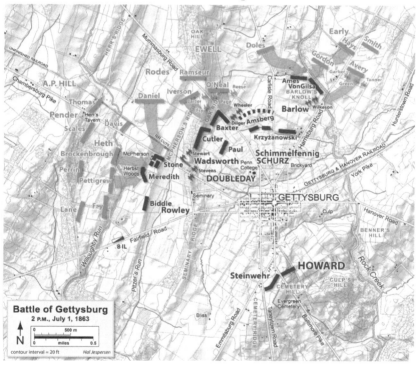

The attack at 2 p.m.

Lee Arrives on the Field

When Lee arrived around 2:30 p.m. and found a major battle in progress, he rescinded his previous order and gave Hill permission to attack. Heth was first in line with fresh brigades at his disposal under Pettigrew and Brockenbrough.

In some of the most intense fighting yet seen in the war, Pettigrew's North Carolina boys pushed the Federal Iron Brigade back to the Lutheran Theological Seminary. The Federal troops to the left on McPherson Ridge were decimated, and the Bucktails came under heavy attack.

Heth united with Major General Robert E. Rodes's division around 3 p.m., attacking with five brigades. During the fighting, a bullet struck Heth in the head, but he was saved by the newspapers he'd stuffed into his overly large hat to make it fit. The general lost consciousness for more than twenty-four hours and thus missed the remainder of the battle. Fragments of his division, under Pettigrew, fought through Pickett's Charge on July 3. Heth recovered sufficiently to command the army's retreat to Virginia.

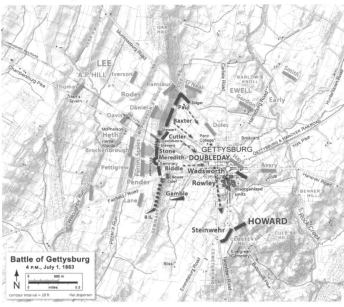

Rodes and Pender break through.

The fourth phase of the battle began at 4 p.m. when Jubal Early's
nfederate division appeared on the battlefield, having moved
rtheast on the Harrisburg Road. Lee ordered a general assault. Early's
n forced the right flank of the Union XI Corps to buckle, which
sed a chain reaction down the Union line, then some two miles in
gth.

The Union troops retreated through the town, taking up positions on
p's Hill and Cemetery Hill, where disarray reigned in the Federal
ks. Thousands of wandering soldiers searched for their units,
ering in small, exhausted groups around their tattered regimental
s. Around 5 o'clock, fortune shined on the Union Army with the
al of Maj. Gen. Winfield Scott Hancock, who was deputized to act
eade's personal representative.

ancock possessed the authority to issue orders in Meade's name
to evaluate the battlefield. A man of decisive action, Hancock
ntly ended the bickering between Doubleday and Howard over what
next by simply assuming command. He ordered Howard to keep
I Corps on Cemetery Hill, sent the I Corps to defend Culp's Hill,
lispatched word to Meade that the troops could retire or stand and
as the ground was "not unfavorable." His decisive action proved
tageous. At roughly the same time Hancock reached the
field, Lee ordered Maj. Gen. Richard Ewell to push the tactical
tage the Confederates held and take both hills.

one of the most controversial moments of the battle, however,
backed down. His troops had fought hard all day, arriving already
sted from hard marching. The general flinched when he saw both
s covered with Union artillery. Additionally, Lee's orders—in a
ng example of his often confusingly polite tone with subordinate
anders—gave Ewell an out. He was told to take the heights "if
able" but to avoid a more general engagement.

t wording in the face of twelve hours of hard fighting in and
the town, would, arguably, have left any commander scratching
ad. Ewell's failure to act ended the day's fighting. The
erates won the day but failed to deliver the death blow.
uently, as the sun set on July 1, the Union had 27,000 men in
n the high ground and approximately eighty-five field pieces.

Richard S. Ewell

Like many of the combatants at Gettysburg, Confederate General Richard S. Ewell was the grandson of a Revolutionary War officer and a West Point graduate (Class of 1840). Ewell's friends called him "Old Baldy" thanks to his early hair loss.

Sewell served on the Santa Fe and Oregon Trails in his early army service. During the Mexican-American War, his bravery at Contreras and Churubusco resulted in a promotion to captain. At Churubusco, he served with Robert E. Lee. After the war, he explored portions of the Gadsden Purchase in the New Mexico Territory but was wounded fighting the Apache in 1859.

Returning to his home state of Virginia, where he was born in 1817, Ewell endured a long recovery but never fully regained his health. Although he held political views generally favorable to the Union, like Lee, he could not bear to fight against his birth state. Ewell resigned his commission on May 7, 1861, to join the Provisional Army of Virginia.

Wounded at Fairfax Court House on May 31, 1861, he was the first Confederate officer of field grade to be wounded during the war. Following a promotion to brigadier general, Ewell commanded a brigade at the First Battle of Bull Run.

Interestingly, within hours of the battle's end, Ewell told President Davis that the South must free its slaves and allow them to fight in the Confederate Army, expressing his willingness to lead African-American troops. Davis dismissed the idea, and the topic was never brought up again.

Ewell proved to be an inspirational leader despite an unassuming appearance and well-known eccentricities. Standing 5'8" with only a fringe of brown hair, the general had eyes that bulged on either side of a beak-like nose. He had an odd habit of letting his head droop to one side and spoke with a whistling lisp. During conversation, Ewell often came out with unintentional non sequiturs and had an impressive command of profanity. Nervous and given to hypochondria, the general slept in odd positions, sometimes wrapped around a stool, and ate a diet composed largely of wheat boiled in milk and sprinkled with sugar.

Oddities aside, however, he performed brilliantly on the field; he was promoted to major general and given a division in January 1862. He worked well with Stonewall Jackson, striking an odd contrast to the pious, stern commander. In his work with Jackson, it became clear that ell only functioned well when given precise instructions, something he uld not receive from Lee at Gettysburg.

After seeing action in numerous battles, Ewell was wounded at wner's Farm on August 28, 1862, by a Minié ball to the left leg. After g undiscovered on the battlefield for several hours, Ewell was taken he field hospital, where doctors amputated the leg. He endured a ful recovery complicated by a fall on Christmas Day due to the poor f his wooden leg. When not in the saddle, he required crutches.

The general returned to fight with Lee at Chancellorsville. In May 3, he was given command of the II Corps and promoted to tenant general. Though he performed well early in the Gettysburg npaign, his failure to capture Cemetery Hill on July 1 tarnished his tation, making him an attractive target for post-war Lee apologists blamed Ewell for the defeat primarily to protect their hero.

His wound and nervous disposition continued to plague Ewell ugh the Battle of the Wilderness in 1864 and the Battle of tsylvania Court House. Lee removed him from field command, ad assigning the general to defend Richmond. Surrounded by on troops after a fire that destroyed a third of the city, Ewell and his were captured only days before Appomattox. The general was held oston Harbor at Fort Warren until July.

When released, Ewell retired to Tennessee. Though his leg stump finally healed, Ewell suffered from numerous other complaints. ve in local education and the Episcopal Church, Ewell led an active ntil he and his wife succumbed to pneumonia within days of each r in January 1872.

Winfield Scott Hancock

Hancock, born in 1824 in Montgomery Square, Pennsylvania, ubtedly prevented a decisive rout of the Union forces on the first f Gettysburg. His decision that day represented but one of many nplary actions in a distinguished career as a military officer and e politician. An 1844 graduate of West Point, Hancock stood eenth in a class of twenty-five. His first posting in the 6th Infantry nent was in the Red River Valley. He saw action in the Mexican-rican War under his namesake, General Winfield Scott, in his y unopposed campaign to take Mexico City. For actions at reras and Churubusco, Hancock received a brevet promotion to ieutenant for meritorious and gallant service.

In 1850, he married Almira Russell. She and the couple's two children accompanied him to his 1855 posting at Fort Myers, Florida. Acting primarily as a quartermaster, Hancock saw no action in the Third Seminole War. Instead, he was sent to Fort Leavenworth, Kansas, and then Utah before being stationed in California, where he remained until the outbreak of the Civil War.

Choosing to remain loyal to the Union, Hancock returned east, receiving a September 1861 promotion to brigadier general and a brigade command under Brig. Gen. William F. Smith. After assuming command of the 1st Division II Corps when Maj. Gen. Israel B. Richardson fell at the Battle of Antietam, Hancock was promoted to major general of volunteers in November 1862.

He suffered an abdominal wound at the Battle of Fredericksburg and a second injury at Chancellorsville, where his division covered Hooker's withdrawal. Upon recovering, Hancock became the commander of the II Corps, participating in the Battle of Gettysburg, where he saw major action on July 2 and faced Pickett's Charge against Cemetery Ridge on July 3.

On the final day of the battle, Hancock, who insisted on remaining in the saddle to rally his troops, was wounded a third time—in the thigh—an injury that would plague him for the remainder of his life. He refused, however, to be removed from the field until the conclusion of the fighting. After recuperating, he commanded the II Corps under Lt. Gen. Ulysses S. Grant in the Overland Campaign despite his impaired mobility.

Hancock saw action at the Battles of the Wilderness, Spotsylvania Courthouse, and Cold Harbor. On August 12, 1864, he was promoted to brigadier general in the regular army. Following a humiliating defeat at Ream's Station during the Siege of Petersburg, Hancock gave up field command in November 1864.

He subsequently performed recruiting work, led the First Veteran Corps, and commanded the troops stationed in the Shenandoah Valley. In 1865, he received a brevet promotion to major general in the regular army. Following the Lincoln assassination on April 14, 1865, Hancock oversaw the execution of the conspirators on July 7.

Hancock's post-war accomplishments were impressive and many, including an 1880 presidential run as a Democrat. A charter director of the National Rifle Association, he was heavily involved with veterans' oups, wrote about his military career, and presided over the funeral of esident Ulysses S. Grant in 1885. Hancock died in 1886 of an fection and complications of diabetes.

Of the many notable men who fought at Gettysburg on both sides, ancock was arguably one of the most dedicated to military and civil rvice. Numerous statues memorialize the general, and his image aced the $2 series of silver certificates issued in 1886.

End of the Day

Had it not been for Hancock's take-charge attitude when he arrived 1 the disorganized battlefield on July 1, the Union Army would have und itself in far worse shape at the end of the day. As it was, the Union oops had been outnumbered and outflanked repeatedly.

By not pressing their advantage, the Confederates left their enemy in 1 unusually strong position for "losers." Around midnight, when Union eneral George Meade joined the Army of the Potomac, he took stock the defensive position at his disposal and decided to stay and fight the xt day.

Confederate General James Longstreet reached Lee's headquarters ar the seminary at approximately 9 p.m. and learned of Lee's plan to the same with considerable alarm. Before the invasion, Lee's stated tent had been to switch to tactical defensive operations on the ground his choosing should he be forced into a major engagement. Now, he d Longstreet that if the Federal forces remained at Gettysburg the next y, the Confederates would attack.

The situation at the end of the first day's fighting continues to provide dder for armchair generals. Without question, had the Confederates ken the high ground and positioned artillery there, the second day of e battle would have turned out far differently. These are the same ilk theorists who insist that had Stonewall Jackson lived to fight at ettysburg, victory would have been gained on day one.

The absence of Jeb Stuart's cavalry deprived Lee of valuable formation and contributed to the accidental start of the battle on the orning of July 1. On the second day, with no cavalry to scout for him, e worked with an uncertain picture of the Union troop positions.

Through the night, the remaining participants on both sides joined e battle, including Johnson and Anderson's division for the South and o of Longstreet's divisions. The Union II and III Corps further engthened the Union position on Cemetery Ridge, with the XII and V

Corps to the east. That left only the Union VI Corps on the march to join the Army of the Potomac.

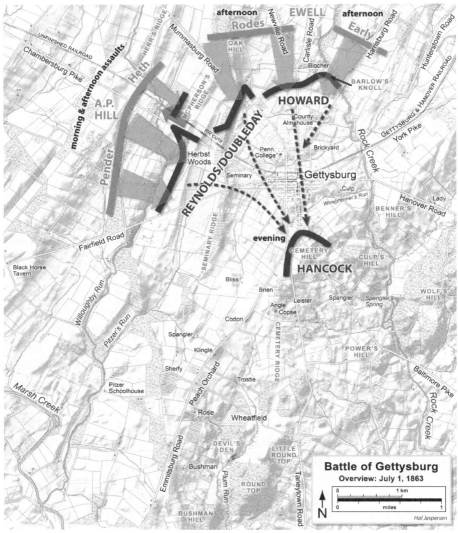

Overview of the first day of the battle.
This file is licensed under the Creative Commons Attribution 3.0 Unported license. Attribution: Map by Hal Jespersen, www.posix.com/CW;
https://commons.wikimedia.org/wiki/File:Gettysburg_Battle_Map_Day1.png

Chapter 4 – Thursday, July 2, 1863

round midnight on July 1, General Meade chose to headquarter in ydia Leister's farmhouse, situated on the southwest slope of Cemetery ill. After consulting with Buford, Hancock, and others, the general iickly reviewed his position during a dawn ride and formulated his efensive plan.

The XI Corps would remain on Cemetery Hill, with the XII Corps ing to Culp's Hill. What remained of the I Corps would take up ation between them. The II Corps under Hancock was moved to emetery Ridge, an elevation Meade intended to further reinforce as esh troops arrived. Big Round Top and Little Round Top anchored ie Union line. All told, Meade deployed six of his seven corps along a ree-mile front that formed a giant fishhook.

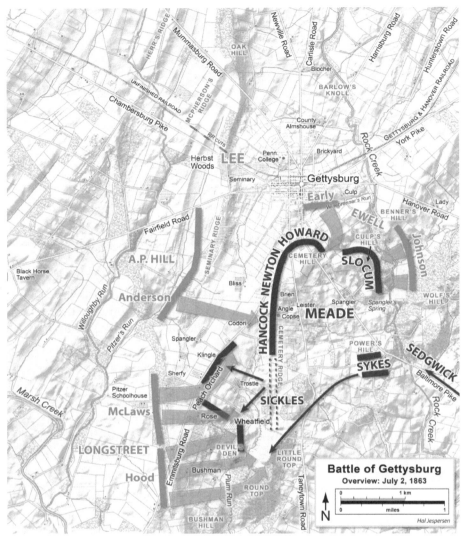

Map of the battle on the second day.
Map by Hal Jespersen, www.posix.com/CW, CC BY 3.0
<https://creativecommons.org/licenses/by/3.0>, via Wikimedia Commons;
https://commons.wikimedia.org/wiki/File:Gettysburg_Battle_Map_Day2.png

Lee's Army of Northern Virginia sat in a roughly parallel position on Seminary Ridge, forming an arc to the north of town. The Confederate II Corps (Ewell) and III Corps (Hill) were on the field, with the I Corps (Longstreet) arriving from Cashtown. The only one of Longstreet's divisions not to fight on July 2 were the men under the command of General George E. Pickett.

Ewell's failure to take either Culp's or Cemetery Hill at the end of the first day of the battle left Lee facing an enemy entrenched on high ground with interior lines ideal for moving reinforcements to strengthen weak spots. At first light, with the plan to attack still central in his thinking, Lee sent a staff engineer to examine the Union left flank.

The officer, Capt. Samuel R. Johnston, delivered a glaringly inaccurate report, claiming that the Union line ran south from Cemetery Ridge along the Emmitsburg Road and ended south of the Codori farm buildings, which were painted red. Johnston also said there were no Union troops on Little Round Top. Based on that flawed intelligence, he formulated his July 2 strategy.

Lee Issues His Orders

At approximately 9 a.m., the Confederate commander had solidified his vision for the day. Longstreet would attack on the Union left, Ewell would make a "demonstration" on the right, and Hill would move against the center. Both Longstreet and Ewell objected.

Longstreet argued for a move around the Union left to break Meade's lines of communication. After all, the general said, the original intent of the invasion had been to enter the enemy's territory and disrupt his operations through a series of harrying defensive battles. For his part, Ewell simply didn't want to move his men from positions they'd fought hard to capture the day before.

Lee ignored the concerns of both men. He felt that the troops could see Longstreet's proposal as a retreat in the face of victory, which would harm morale. As for Ewell, his instructions left him free to execute a real attack if the opportunity arose, which should satisfy the fighting spirit of his men. Lee insisted that Cemetery Hill must be captured to give the Confederates a commanding position over the town of Gettysburg, allowing them to disrupt the Federal supply lines and control the road to Washington, D.C.

When Longstreet realized that Lee would not change his mind, he tried to delay the start of the battle, protesting that John Bell Hood's division had not completely arrived on the field and Pickett was a half-day's march away. Lee insisted the attack proceed without Pickett but agreed that Longstreet could wait for Hood's last brigade. Lee also arranged for Maj. Gen. Richard H. Anderson's division from Hill's III Corps to cooperate with Longstreet.

After all the well-mannered bickering was resolved, Longstreet, with two divisions, was to straddle the Emmitsburg Road with Hood on the eastern side and Lafayette McLaws to the west, forming perpendicular lines. The goal was to collapse the Union defenders against themselves in an oblique or angled attack, leading to the capture of Cemetery Hill. Meanwhile, Anderson's division would stand ready to enter the fight at the center of the line.

Not realizing that Longstreet intended to put off the attack as long as possible, Lee rode to Ewell's headquarters and returned at 11 a.m. to find Longstreet right where he'd left him. Lee ordered his reluctant subordinate to attack at once. Dutifully, Longstreet began the march southeast, only to halt south of the Fairfield Road when advance units reported the presence of Union troops on Little Round Top.

This was the first indicator of Lee's faulty intelligence and the significance that misunderstanding would have for the day's events. Rather than the Federal left flank hanging in the air as Lee believed, the Federals held a line running the length of Cemetery Ridge anchored by Little Round Top.

Lee's plan was doomed before a single shot was fired. Longstreet's troops attacking up the road would face at least two Union corps on their right flank, with guns on the heights. Then, General Daniel E. Sickles and his Union III Corps altered the situation to the even greater detriment of the Southerners.

James Longstreet

Longstreet, born in Edgefield District, South Carolina, on January 8, 1821, was of Dutch descent. Described by his father as having a "rock-like" character, the boy picked up the lifelong nickname "Pete" after St. Peter, the rock upon which the Christian church was built.

Sent to live with relatives in Augusta, Georgia, Longstreet attended a neighboring military academy. Known for his rough manners and coarse language, Longstreet never cursed in the presence of women. He held no political convictions. His uncle, Augustus Longstreet, however, was a states' rights advocate who passed a love of whiskey and cards on to his nephew.

Entering West Point in 1838, Longstreet consistently ranked in the bottom third of his class. He absorbed significant tactical understanding, however—lessons evident in his emphasis on swift movement, protected interior lines, and strategic troop placements over showy encounters. He raduated 54th of 56 in the Class of 1842.

While serving in Missouri with the 4th Infantry, Longstreet efriended Ulysses S. Grant and may have been a member of the edding party when Grant married Longstreet's fourth cousin, Julia ent. From Missouri, Longstreet went to Louisiana, Florida, and Texas efore serving in the Mexican-American War with the 8th Infantry.

At the Battle of Chapultepec, Longstreet was wounded in the thigh, lling with the regimental colors in his hand, which he passed to Lt. eorge Pickett. Unable to return home until December, Longstreet imediately married Louise Garland. With her, he fathered ten ildren.

In 1850, Longstreet became Chief Commissary for the Department Texas, a position he resigned in 1851 to return to the 8th Infantry. He rved on the frontier near Fredericksburg, Texas, and was posted in buquerque, New Mexico, when the first shot of the Civil War was ed. Longstreet resigned his commission and joined the Confederate ites Army.

Immediately promoted to brigadier general and given command of ee Virginia infantry regiments, Longstreet saw heavy action in the first) years of the war. He rose to the rank of major general in command a division in the Army of Northern Virginia.

In January 1862, the general suffered immense personal tragedy when ee of his children died of scarlet fever in rapid succession. Afterward, ngstreet became withdrawn, rarely drinking or playing cards with his cers, turning instead to religion for comfort.

By July 1863, he was a seasoned commander who enjoyed a close sonal friendship with Lee. Regardless of their feeling for one another, vever, the men disagreed at Gettysburg. Critics claim that Longstreet's lys on the second day led to the Confederate defeat.

Though not victorious in the pivotal battle, Longstreet survived the and a treason conviction to become a prosperous businessman. In 0, he was even appointed ambassador to the Ottoman Empire by sident Rutherford B. Hayes. Longstreet retired to his Georgia farm in 4, where he penned his memoirs over five years. Nothing that he te swayed his detractors.

he general died in January 1904, days shy of his eighty-third iday. He left behind a second wife forty-two years his junior who nantly defended his reputation until her own death in 1962.

Longstreet was one of only a handful of general officers from the Civil War to see the dawn of the 20th century.

While his actions at Gettysburg remain a matter of lengthy debate, one thing can be said with certainty: he did not expect to encounter Sickles' men in the Peach Orchard after a day of circuitous maneuvering to avoid observation by the enemy.

Sickles Makes a Unilateral Decision

Early on July 2, Meade had ordered General Daniel E. Sickles to position his men on Cemetery Ridge with the II Corps on his right and Little Round Top on the left. As the morning wore on, however, Sickles became fixated on a Peach Orchard in front of his placement, owned by the Sherfy family. At 11 a.m., Sickles rode to Meade's headquarters to request permission to move to the Peach Orchard, complaining that he'd been assigned a poor position. Meade, angry but calm, repeated his original orders. Having been forced to cede high ground at Chancellorsville, which was then used by artillery to bombard his forces, Sickles, however, could not shake the belief that he faced a crushing defeat at the hands of the enemy. Sickles ultimately decided—against orders—to occupy the orchard, ordering his two divisions to move 1,500 yards west of Cemetery Ridge into the orchard. In doing so, he put himself in a position to be attacked on multiple sides along lines too long for the men under his command to defend.

Though correct in his belief that there would be a significant Confederate assault in that area, Sickles, a politician with no military training, was mistaken that the Peach Orchard was a superior placement. He deployed his troops at a sharp angle—a salient—difficult to defend against a determined foe.

He exposed the Federal division along the Emmitsburg Road, under the command of Maj. Gen. Andrew A. Humphreys, to interlocking Confederate fire without sufficient artillery to respond. Maj. Gen. David B. Birney's division was spread out from the Peach Orchard to the Wheatfield and all the way to Devil's Den without enough men to cover the front. And, worse yet, Sickles left the Taneytown Road unguarded, imperiling one of Meade's essential lines of communication.

Longstreet Forced to Countermarch

After spying Federals on the summit of Little Round Top, Longstreet countermarched his columns. He adopted a serpentine route, using the intervening ridges to screen his troops from the Federal observers.

onsequently, he didn't reach his position until four in the afternoon. istead of the empty fields and orchards Longstreet expected, he found ickles's Union III Corps in front of him on the Emmitsburg Road.

General Hood argued for a change in the Confederate battle plan, insidering the unexpected developments. He wanted to swing around ittle Round Top and attack the Federals from the rear. Longstreet fused. Although frustrated with Lee's refusal to reconceive his strategy the light of what was now clearly bad intelligence, he ordered an imediate attack.

Hood was to lead the action, followed by McLaws and Anderson, oving from south to north. Still adamant that the plan was a mistake, ood lodged a formal protest even as he prepared to engage the ederals. Before the assault, Longstreet opened the engagement with a irty-minute artillery barrage comprised of thirty-six guns. The battery t the Federal soldiers in the Peach Orchard hard and hammered their itteries on Houck's Ridge.

John Bell Hood

John Bell Hood, born in Kentucky in 1831, was an 1853 graduate of 'est Point known by the nickname "Sam." He nearly missed graduating ogether, running up 196 demerits in his final year at the academy.

Commissioned a brevet second lieutenant, he served as a cavalry ficer in California and Texas, the latter under Lt. Col. Robert E. Lee. roughout his military career, Hood was plagued by a series of wounds at began with a Comanche arrow through the hand while on patrol itside Fort Mason in 1857.

After Ft. Sumter, Hood resigned his commission and offered his rvices to Texas, where he joined the army as a captain. Soon promoted major, Hood and his cavalry command headed east to see tinguished service in Virginia before becoming colonel of the 4th :xas Infantry on September 20, 1861.

In March 1862, Hood was promoted to brigadier general in charge of igades comprised primarily of Texas regiments. Ever eager to rsonally lead his troops in battle, Hood was an aggressive commander io honed his command into an elite unit. At the Battle of Gaines' Mill June 27, he led a charge that broke the Union line. The victory cost : Texans dearly, however. More than 400 of Hood's men—and most his officers—were killed or wounded, a sight that reduced the general tears.

In July, Hood's brigade was moved to Longstreet's corps and reduced from five to two brigades—the Texas brigade and Evander M. Law's Mississippians. At Second Bull Run, Hood's attack on the Federal left forced a retreat at the cost of more than a thousand casualties.

At Antietam, Hood relieved Stonewall Jackson's corps, turning back an assault by the Union I Corps that cost the division another thousand casualties. Though the price was bloody, the action resulted in Hood's elevation to major general in October 1862. His troops saw little action at either Fredericksburg or Chancellorsville, but fate awaited them at Gettysburg.

During the attack on Little Round Top on July 2, an artillery shell incapacitated Hood. His arm was not amputated, but Hood dealt with limited mobility for the rest of his life. He retained a decent grip with his left hand and motion at the elbow but could not raise his arm from the shoulder.

Recovering in Richmond, the tall, thin Hood with his blue eyes and blond beard made quite the impression on the ladies. He proposed to Sally Buchanan Preston, but she was noncommittal. Disappointed, Hood rejoined his men for the Battle of Chickamauga, September 18-20, 1863. On the 20th, he was injured again, a wound that forced the amputation of his right leg four inches below the hip.

The attending surgeon, convinced the general would die, loaded the severed leg onto the ambulance so it could be buried with Hood. Promoted to lieutenant general, Hood spent part of his second recuperation in Richmond, where he tried again to court Sally Preston. By February, he had a tentative "yes" from the girl, but as her family disapproved, he returned to the war in the spring of 1864 as a single man.

Although he had to be strapped in the saddle, Hood rode as far as twenty miles a day. An orderly stayed nearby, however, with the general's crutches ready. His artificial leg, along with at least two spares, had been given to Hood by the men of the Texas Brigade, who collected more than $3,000 in one day to aid their injured leader.

Hood saw serious action for the remainder of the war, fighting against Union General William T. Sherman's troops in the Atlanta Campaign and the March to the Sea. Assigned to the Trans-Mississippi Theater in March 1865, Hood surrendered in Natchez, Mississippi, receiving parole on Mary 31, 1865.

Following the war, Hood worked as a cotton broker in Louisiana. There, he finally married, but not to the elusive Sally. Hood and his wife, Anna Marie Hennan, had eleven children over ten years. Their family included three sets of twins. Philanthropic by nature, Hood worked to raise money for widows, orphans, and other wounded war veterans. He began but never finished his memoirs.

In 1879, an outbreak of yellow fever claimed the lives of Hood (age forty-eight), his wife, and their oldest daughter. The Texas Brigade Association supported the remaining ten children, who were adopted into seven families, for over twenty years.

The Attack Begins

As Hood protested the planned attack with Longstreet, Meade caught up with Sickles near Peach Orchard and delivered a blistering verbal reprimand emblematic of his famous temper. Sickles offered to return to Cemetery Ridge just as Longstreet's guns opened fire. Meade had no choice but to order Sickles to stay put and wait to be reinforced.

Hood's division deployed in two lines on the southern end of Seminary Ridge, with Brigadier General Jerome B. Robertson's Texas Brigade on the front left. Evander M. Law was positioned to the right front, George T. Anderson to the left rear, and Henry L. Benning to the right rear.

At 4:30 p.m., Hood ordered the Texas Brigade forward. Longstreet had instructed him to wheel left after crossing the Emmitsburg Road and then move north. Within minutes, however, while sitting astride his horse on Slyder Lane, an artillery shell exploded over Hood. The injury to the general's left arm was so severe he was removed from the field. His leaderless division continued moving east.

Several factors now came into play all at once. Regiments of the Union III Corps in the area known as Devil's Den threatened Hood's right flank. Law's brigade became distracted pursuing the 2nd U.S. Sharpshooters on Slyder Farm, pulling the Confederates to the right. The rough terrain fractured troop alignments, and Law, who had no idea he now commanded the division, failed to bring the situation under control. Consequently, the advance split, with the 1st Texas, 3rd Arkansas, 44th and 48th Alabama moving toward Devil's Den. Law aimed the remaining five regiments toward Big and Little Round Top.

Devil's Den

The Devil's Den, an area littered with boulders, sits at the south end of Houck's Ridge. It anchored the III Corps line on the extreme left, where 2,200 men awaited the advancing Confederates. Union Brigadier General J.H. Hobard Ward commanded the position.

When the 3rd Arkansas and 1st Texas pushed through Rose Woods, they encountered Ward's men directly. The Federals had no time to erect defenses and stood facing their opponents for more than an hour of unusually vicious fighting. In only the first half hour, the 20th Indiana lost 50 percent of its men.

At the same time, two regiments of Law's brigade moved toward Big and Little Round Top through Plum Run Valley, where they menaced Ward's flank. They concentrated their attack against the 4th Maine and 124th New York, which protected the 4th New York Independent Battery firing on the Confederates from the heights.

Ward was forced to move the 99th Pennsylvania from his far right to shore up his left flank. Colonel Augustus Van Horne Ellis of the 124th New York and Major James Cromwell mounted their horses and led a charge down Houck's Ridge through the Triangular Field, repulsing the 1st Texas and moving the line back 200 yards.

The Texans rallied, however, unleashing a volley of fire that killed both Ellis and Cromwell and forced the New York troops back to their original positions. Of the 283 men who followed their officers down the slope, only a hundred returned. The Federals managed to hold the crest, however, due to the timely arrival of reinforcements from the 99th Pennsylvania.

In the second wave of the Southern attack, Benning and Anderson hit Ward's right flank, where a gap in the line had formed around the brigade commanded by Régis de Trobriand. Anderson's men converged on the southern edge of the area known as the Wheatfield, forcing the Union soldiers to fight from behind piles of their dead and wounded. The Southerners were forced to fall back, and Anderson suffered a leg wound that caused him to be removed from the field.

The 2nd and 17th Georgia moved around Ward's flank through Plum Run Valley, where they faced blistering fire from the guns atop Little Round Top and the 99th Pennsylvania. In a scramble for reinforcements, the 40th New York and 6th New Jersey were pulled from the Wheatfield and sent to protect Ward's flank in Plum Run alley.

There, they met the Confederates on a rocky piece of ground now nown as the Slaughter Pen. As a testament to the bloody fighting of the econd day, soldiers called Plum Run Valley the Valley of Death.

The Federal line along Houck's Ridge was collapsing, imperiling the 0th New York. This did not stop the Federals from attacking the onfederates seven times among the boulders strewn in the Slaughter en and Devil's Den. Ultimately, the 40th had no choice but to fall back, rotected by the 6th New Jersey laying down covering fire.

In the end, Ward could not hold his position and retreated, allowing ood's troops to take Devil's Den and the southern end of Houk's idge. The fighting then became concentrated on the northwest in Rose Voods and the Wheatfield, while, to the east, Law's five regiments oved against Little Round Top.

Little Round Top

Had Sickles not moved the III Corps into the Peach Orchard, he ould have been in a position to defend Little Round Top at the south d of Cemetery Ridge. When Meade learned that Sickles had sobeyed his orders, he sent Brigadier General Gouverneur K. Warren, s chief engineer, to remedy the situation.

Standing on the summit of Little Round Top, Warren saw the sun inting on Southern bayonets to the southwest. A Confederate assault as imminent. The general sent for help from any unit available. Major eneral George Sykes, in command of the Union V Corps, answered.

A messenger dispatched by Sykes to order Brigadier General James arnes to move his 1st Division to Little Round Top first encountered e commander of the III Brigade, Colonel Strong Vincent. nderstanding the gravity of the situation, Vincent took the initiative and dered four regiments to the hill without waiting for instructions from arnes.

Strong Vincent

Strong Vincent, born in Waterford, Pennsylvania, in 1837, was a arvard-educated lawyer, graduating in 1859. He joined the ennsylvania Militia at the start of the war as a first lieutenant but was omoted to lieutenant colonel of the 83rd Pennsylvania Infantry in ptember 1861. He assumed command of the regiment as a colonel in ne 1862.

At Gettysburg, the 26-year-old commanded the 3rd Brigade, 1st Division, V Corps of the Army of the Potomac. Knowing his wife was pregnant with their first child, he wrote that, should he be killed, she must remember he died in service to "the most righteous cause that ever widowed a woman."

Although much has been written about Joshua Lawrence Chamberlain and the 20th Maine that day on Little Round Top, Vincent's valor is unquestioned. In the heat of the fighting, as the Union line was in danger of breaking, Vincent climbed atop a large boulder and admonished his men not to give an inch, emphasizing his words with a riding crop given to him by his wife. A bullet caught him in the thigh and groin. Carried from the field to a nearby farmhouse, Vincent died five days later. Meade promoted him to brigadier general on the evening of July 2, but the gravely injured man likely never knew of the honor. Sadly, his infant daughter was born two months later but lived only a year. She is buried next to Vincent in Erie, Pennsylvania.

Vincent Reinforces Little Round Top

Upon arrival, the four regiments Vincent ordered to Little Round Top took immediate fire from Confederate batteries. Starting on the western slope of the hill and moving counterclockwise, Vincent positioned the 44th New York, the 83rd Pennsylvania, and the 20th Maine. Vincent ordered Colonel Joshua Lawrence Chamberlain and the boys of the 20th Maine to hold the southern slope at the end of the line no matter what the Confederates threw at them. Chamberlain had 385 men at his disposal to make his stand.

Joshua Lawrence Chamberlain

Chamberlain's actions at Gettysburg immortalized his name in the history of the battle. He was born in 1828 in Brewer, Maine, and his ancestors fought in the French and Indian War, the American Revolution, and the War of 1812. Named Lawrence Joshua, Chamberlain, who planned to become a clergyman, changed the order of his name to emphasize the biblical "Joshua."

The eldest of five children, Joshua worked in the family's endeavors, principally farming and logging. His father, James, wanted to see his son pursue a military career. His mother, Sarah, favored a religious life for the boy. Both believed their child possessed the natural qualities of a leader.

Chamberlain set his sights on attending Bowdoin College, teaching imself Greek and honing his Latin during 1846 ahead of his entrance pplication. Ultimately, he mastered seven languages. Accepted in ebruary 1847, Chamberlain overcame a stutter so completely he would) on to be regarded as an orator of considerable skill.

Active in church work throughout his college years, Chamberlain nrolled in Bangor Theological Seminary after graduating from Bowdoin 1852. He married Fanny Adams in 1855, returning to Bowdoin that ll as an instructor and then professor. At the outbreak of the Civil War, e was granted a leave of absence, ostensibly to study in Europe. Instead, e enlisted as a lieutenant colonel and ultimately became colonel of the)th Maine.

For his gallant defense of Little Round Top on July 2, 1863, hamberlain received the Medal of Honor in 1893. After Gettysburg, he as awarded a brigade command before the Siege of Petersburg in 1864. t the Second Battle of Petersburg, a bullet pierced his right hip and oin, but Chamberlain drove his sword into the ground and held mself upright to rally his troops before finally collapsing from blood ss.

Though the wound was judged mortal, Chamberlain survived. He ceived a battlefield promotion to brigadier general, recuperated, and turned to his command in November. In 1865, during an engagement n Quaker Road, Chamberlain was shot again in the left arm and chest, arly requiring the amputation of the limb. Again, he stayed on the ld, encouraging his men to move forward. For these actions, he ceived a presidential promotion to major general.

In the morning hours of April 9, 1865, a Confederate staff officer pproached Chamberlain with Lee's offer to surrender the Army of orthern Virginia. The next day, Chamberlain was selected to preside as e Confederate infantry paraded into Appomattox for the formal rrender that would take place on April 12. As the Southerners epared to hand over their weapons and colors, Chamberlain ordered men to attention and "carry arms" in respect for their defeated emy.

In the twenty major battles in which he served, Chamberlain received ur citations for bravery, suffered six wounds, and had six horses shot m under him. Returning to Maine after the war, he served four terms the state's governor before returning to Bowdoin as the school's president from 1871 to 1883, resigning only when his health declined due to his wartime injuries. He subsequently practiced law and engaged in various business pursuits, including Florida real estate.

Chamberlain returned to Gettysburg many times after the battle, making his last trip to Pennsylvania in 1913 to plan the 50th anniversary commemoration of the engagement. Ill health kept him from attending the event two months later. He died in Portland, Maine, in 1914 at 85. His death was ruled a complication of the wound he suffered at Petersburg, making him, in the eyes of many, the last casualty of the American Civil War.

Confrontation on Little Round Top

General Evander M. Law, in command of the Alabama Brigade, sent the 4th, 15th, and 47th Alabama and the 4th and 5th Texas to take Little Round Top. The troops had marched more than twenty miles to reach the battlefield on a hot day. They were tired and out of water.

Striking the Federals on the crest, the attackers were repelled by them on the first volley. Regrouping, the 15th Alabama under Colonel William C. Oates shifted right to determine the location of the Federals' left flank—Chamberlain's position, which he held along with the 83rd Pennsylvania to his right.

Observing the Confederate move, Chamberlain elongated his position until the defenders on the hill stood in a single-file line. During a break in the assault, he ordered his troops at the far south end to swing back at an angle to the main line and stop the Southern flanking attempt.

Over an hour and a half, the 20th Maine held off two Confederate charges. In an audacious move, Chamberlain, with dwindling numbers and little to no ammunition, ordered a bayonet charge. His left flank advanced and wheeled to the right. When they came in line with the rest of the regiment, the rest of the troops charged—in effect, closing the door.

By pairing a frontal assault with a flanking maneuver, Chamberlain stopped and captured almost all the 15th Alabama. As the remaining Southerners retreated, Company B of the 20th Maine under Captain Walter G. Morrill and a handful of 2nd U.S. Sharpshooters kept up a volley of rifle fire. The effect was utter confusion in the Confederate ranks.

Elsewhere on the hill, however, the Alabama troops delivered punishing attacks on the Union left, while the 4th and 5th Texas saulted the right. Vincent received a mortal wound during one of the larges, and command passed to Colonel James C. Rice.

The 140th New York arrived to assist in the defense of the hill, along ith four guns of Battery D, 5th U.S. Artillery that were hauled up the ocky slopes by hand. However, the artillerymen, under the command of t. Charles E. Hazlett, faced constant sniper fire that hampered their ovements. Additionally, they could not sufficiently lower the barrels of eir pieces to gain a proper firing angle against the infantry attacks.

The arrival of the fresh New York troops saved the day. The Union ld Little Round Top and would control the position for the remainder the battle. Southern sharpshooters continued to pick off Union troops 1 the heights, however, killing General David Weed, who commanded brigade of the Union V Corps. Hazlett, a friend of Weed's, moved to omfort the fallen man only to die by a sniper's bullet himself.

Skirmishes on Little Round Top continued into the evening. The one breastworks on the hill constructed by the Federals to defend the osition are still visible today. The hill was the starting point of the nion counterattack. At dusk, Brigadier General Samuel W. Crawford d the 3rd Division of the V Corps in an assault toward the Wheatfield.

The Wheatfield

In conceiving the day's plan of attack, Lee intended for Hood and aj. Gen. Lafayette McLaws to launch a simultaneous attack. ongstreet, however, held McLaws back. By 5 p.m., with the enemy fully igaged in front of Hood's division, Longstreet saw that the troops were earing their limit.

McLaws's men on Warfield Ridge were positioned in twin lines of o brigades each. Brig. Gen. William Barksdale faced the Peach rchard on the front left with Brig. Gen. Joseph B. Kershaw on his ght, and Brig. Gen. William T. Wofford was behind Barksdale with rig. Gen. Paul Jones Semmes on his right.

Longstreet ordered the deployment of Kershaw's brigade, with arksdale to follow in sequence. Some of the bloodiest fighting of the econd day took place in the Wheatfield and the Peach Orchard.

John Rose owned the three major geographic features of the area esignated as the "Wheatfield." These included the field itself ncompassing twenty acres), Rose Woods on the west side of the field, d a small rise called Stony Hill on the west. Houck's Ridge lay to the utheast and Devil's Den to the south.

For two hours in the Wheatfield, eleven brigades engaged in a series of attacks and counterattacks, earning the ground the name "Bloody Wheatfield."

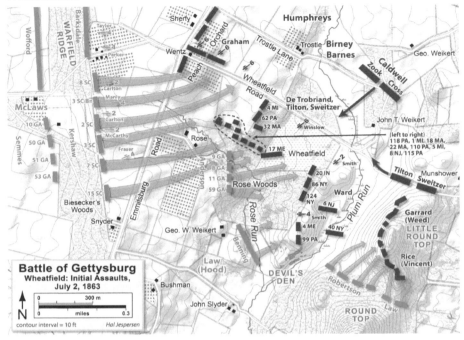

Initial assaults on Wheatfield.
Map by Hal Jespersen, www.posix.com/CW, CC BY 3.0
<https://creativecommons.org/licenses/by/3.0>, via Wikimedia Commons;
https://commons.wikimedia.org/wiki/File:Gettysburg_Day2_Wheatfield1.png

The first confrontation occurred when Anderson's brigade, as part of Hood's assault on Houck's Ridge, met the 18th Maine. The Federals, assisted by battery under Winslow, held and forced the Confederates to fall back.

By 5:30 p.m., as the Southern troops under Kershaw neared the Rose farmhouse, two brigades under colonels William S. Tilton and Jacob B. Sweitzer (part of Brig. Gen. James Barnes's 1st Division, V Corps) had reinforced Stony Hill.

The 17th Maine held again against the Confederates, but Barnes chose to withdraw 300 yards to the north, assuming a position near the Wheatfield Road. This forced the 17th Maine to pull back as well, allowing the Southerners to take Stony Hill and enter the Wheatfield en masse.

This area of the battlefield had been disorganized since Sickles made the poorly conceived decision to move to the Peach Orchard. Meade ordered General Winfield Scott Hancock to pull a division from the II Corps to reinforce the III. Hancock chose Brig. Gen. John C. Caldwell's 1st Division, then in a reserve location at the back of Cemetery Ridge.

Caldwell arrived around 6 p.m. with three brigades (Zook, Kelly, and Cross) and one in reserve (Brooke). Kelly's troops, known as the Irish Brigade, reclaimed Stony Hill while Cross pushed the Southerners out of the Wheatfield. In the fighting, both Zook and Cross were wounded and later died.

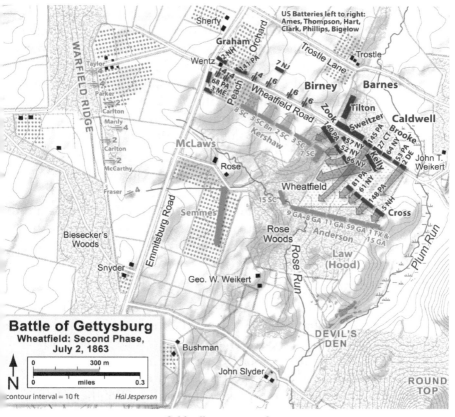

Caldwell counterattacks.

When Cross's brigade ran low on ammunition, it was relieved by Brooke's men. The Union hold on the Peach Orchard fell apart, however, and the Confederates under Wofford once again took Stony Hill and pressed the Union flank in the Wheatfield. Brooke retreated into Rose Woods while Sweitzer's men slowed the Confederate attack in brutal hand-to-hand fighting.

With the Wheatfield once again in Union hands, reinforcements under Brig. Gen. Romeyn B. Ayres arrived (2nd Division, V Corps). As these Union men advanced, the Southerners came over Stony Hill and through Rose Woods in a swarm, flanking them and forcing an orderly retreat to Little Round Top.

This last Confederate attack of the day, around 7:30 p.m., continued through the Wheatfield, past Houck's Ridge, and into the Valley of Death. A counterattack was launched by Brig. Gen. Samuel W. Crawford from the north side of Little Round Top, led by a brigade of men under Colonel William McCandless that included a company of Gettysburg men. They drove the Southerners, now completely worn out from the day's fighting, back through the Wheatfield to Stony Hill before Crawford pulled back to the eastern boundary of the field. The area would, mercifully, remain quiet on the third day of the battle.

Six Confederate brigades fought thirteen Union brigades in the Bloody Wheatfield. A total of 20,244 men were involved, with a casualty rate of 30 percent. The wounded who tried to escape to Plum Run made the waters of the small stream run red. The vicious day of back-and-forth possession took such a heavy psychological toll on the troops that this small portion of the larger battle carried strong significance among Civil War veterans.

Peach Orchard

While Kershaw's right wing focused on assaulting the Wheatfield, the left hit Brig. Gen. Charles K. Graham's Pennsylvania troops, who were supported by thirty artillery pieces from the III Corps. The Confederates, mainly from South Carolina, endured heavy volleys until someone shouted a command to turn right into the Wheatfield. No such order had been issued. The mistake subjected the Southern left flank to brutal fire from the Union batteries. Hundreds fell to their deaths under the guns.

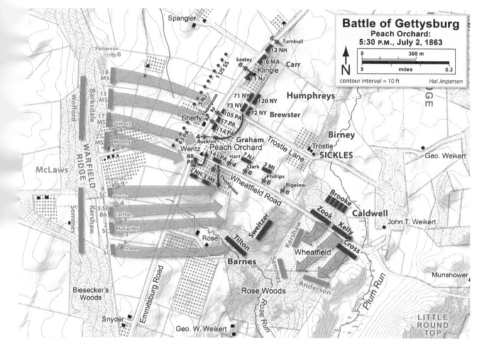

Peach Orchard positions.
Map by Hal Jespersen, www.posix.com/CW, CC BY 3.0
<https://creativecommons.org/licenses/by/3.0>, via Wikimedia Commons;
https://commons.wikimedia.org/wiki/File:Gettysburg_Day2_Peach_Orchard1.png

At the same time, the Confederate brigades on McLaws's left charged the Peach Orchard. General Barksdale, on horseback with sword drawn, led the attack. Roughly a thousand Union troops defended the position in a 500-yard line that ran north adjacent to the Emmitsburg Road and the lane of Abraham Trostle's farm.

With 1,600 Mississippi men behind him, Barksdale flanked the Union troops. Regiment by regiment, the line collapsed as the Federals fled toward Cemetery Ridge. Twice, Union General Graham's horses went down. Finally, the commander was hit by a bullet and shell fragment, leading to his capture by the 21st Mississippi.

Sickles, headquartered in the Trostle barn, was moving his men to the rear when a cannonball hit his right leg. Carried from the field on a stretcher, sitting upright and smoking a cigar, he attempted to rally his men. That evening, Sickles lost his leg, and command of the III Corps passed to General Birney.

The Union guns, endangered by infantry attacks in the Peach Orchard and Wheatfield Road, withdrew—some being dragged from the field while still firing. At the Trostle farmhouse, the 21st Mississippi captured three of the 9th Massachusetts Light Artillery's field pieces.

Late Evening Actions

Major General Richard H. Anderson's Confederate division (III Corps) attacked at 6 p.m. with five brigades. Humphrey could not maintain his position on the Emmitsburg Road, sealing the fate of the Union III Corps, though the general remained astride his mount and ensured a retreat in good order.

Meanwhile, on Cemetery Ridge, Meade and Hancock supervised a scramble of reinforcements. Meade sent almost all the men at his disposal to face Longstreet's attack, weakening the center of his line.

Hancock took Colonel George L. Willard's brigade (II Corps) to face Barksdale's Confederates on Seminary Ridge, driving the Mississippi men back to the Emmitsburg Road. Barksdale suffered multiple wounds in the fighting—a shot to the left knee, a cannonball to the left foot, and a bullet to the chest. When he finally fell from his horse, his troops had no choice but to leave him. He died the following morning in a Union field hospital.

Riding north in search of more reinforcements, Hancock detected a gap in the Union line, which the Confederates were set to exploit. He met the threat with the 1st Minnesota, ordering them to attack and seize the enemy flag. The Federal troops fixed bayonets and charged, forcing a Confederate retreat, but at the cost of an 82 percent casualty rate.

The Confederate brigade under Brig. Gen. Ambrose Wright advanced beyond Cemetery Ridge for a time, although many historians dispute the general's claim. Wright later told Lee that advancing to that point had been accomplished with relative ease but holding the position had been much harder. Some theories posit that Lee's conversation with Wright about the ease of his advance could have colored Lee's thinking ahead of Pickett's disastrous charge on the third day.

Around 4 p.m., Confederate General Ewell had begun an artillery barrage that inflicted light damage on the Union right flank but cost Ewell his most effective artillery officer, Maj. Joseph W. Latimer, who died of his wounds months later at only nineteen.

At 7 p.m., Ewell finally mounted an infantry assault, and around 8 p.m., two of Jubal Early's brigades reached East Cemetery Hill, only to driven back by Federal reinforcements.

On Culp's Hill, men of the Federal XII Corps under Brig. Gen. George S. Greene inflicted heavy casualties on the Confederates under Maj. Gen. Edward "Allegheny" Johnson from behind entrenched breastworks. The costly attack gained only insignificant portions of the Union line.

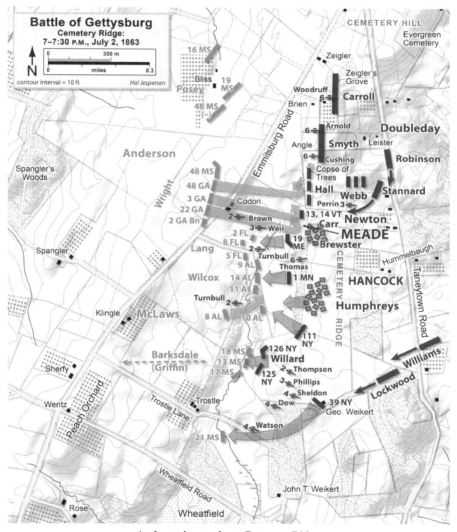

Anderson's assault on Cemetery Ridge.
*Map by Hal Jespersen, www.posix.com/CW, CC BY 3.0
<https://creativecommons.org/licenses/by/3.0>, via Wikimedia Commons;
https://commons.wikimedia.org/wiki/File:Gettysburg_Day2_Cemetery_Ridge.png*

Day Two Comes to an End

At 10:30 p.m., the second day of the Battle of Gettysburg finally ended, the sounds of the night punctuated by the pitiful cries of the wounded and dying men still lying on the field. Though Meade had taken a pummeling, that night he decided to hold his position and await fresh Confederate attacks the coming day. The Union general believed that should his opponent attack on the third day, the confrontation would be at the center of the line, as assaults on the right and left flanks had already failed.

In Lee's headquarters, distress reigned over the failure to rout the Federals. Still, the commander of the Army of Northern Virginia believed that by continuing to attack on the following day, victory was within his grasp. That confidence would prove to be ill-fated.

Chapter 5 – Friday, July 3, 1863, and Beyond

Around midnight on July 2, Meade met with his senior officers at his headquarters, still located in the Leister farmhouse. The general put three questions to the group, recorded by his chief of staff, Maj. Gen. Daniel A. Butterfield. Should the army stay or withdraw? The generals said stay. Should the army attack or wait for Lee to make his next move? After considerable discussion, most wanted to remain on the defensive. Finally, contingent on the previous decision, Meade asked how long they should wait. The consensus was twenty-four hours.

For his part, Lee worked alone that night, not consulting with his subordinates. The general decided to launch fresh attacks on the Union flanks, ordering assaults on both positions to begin in the early morning. Consequently, the Confederate cannon opened fire at 4:30 a.m. in a thunderous barrage.

As ordered, Ewell, reinforced overnight so that his forces were almost doubled, attacked. He did not know, however, that the Union XII Corps had been moved to face him along with a brigade from the VI Corps. The charging Confederates faced a solid wall of Federal fire that shattered their ranks. The Union right flank on Culp's Hill held.

As the firing died down, Lt. Col. Charles R. Mudge, commander of the 2nd Massachusetts, received a garbled order. The intent had been for his unit to probe the Confederate position at Spangler's Spring, but the colonel believed he received a directive to launch a full-scale attack.

Even though he characterized the directive as tantamount to murder, Mudge ordered an advance into the open field. The Confederates, positioned behind stone walls, decimated the Federals, with Mudge himself suffering a mortal wound.

From his position on Seminary Ridge, Lee could hear the fighting on Culp's Hill. In short order, he learned that the Federals had taken the advantage there and Longstreet had made no move against the Union left. Lee assumed that if Meade had reinforced his right flank, he must have done the same on the left. Did that not indicate the weakest point in his enemy's line could be found in the center?

Lee considered moving against Cemetery Ridge, and Longstreet once again objected, saying that not even 15,000 men could overcome the Union center. Lee listened but did not change his mind, opting instead for an attack that has become infamous as "Pickett's Charge."

George Pickett

George Pickett, born in Richmond, Virginia, on January 16, 1825, was a career military officer before accepting a commission with the Confederate States Army. Though he had studied law at an early age, he accepted an appointment to West Point at age seventeen. Popular and mischievous, he was known for his pranks on fellow classmen, for which he earned countless demerits. He graduated last in the Class of 1846.

Pickett gained national recognition during the Mexican-American War when he carried the American flag over the wall at the Battle of Chapultepec in 1847. Pickett then fought his way to the roof and unfurled the colors. He received brevet promotions and commendations for gallant and meritorious conduct.

Pickett served on the Texas frontier and in the Washington Territory, where he married his second wife, Morning Mist, a member of the Haida tribe. She died in childbirth, but her infant son, James Tilton Pickett, lived. Known as "Jimmy," he died of tuberculosis in Portland, Oregon, in 1889 at age thirty-two.

After Fort Sumter, Pickett resigned his US Army commission. Seeing early service in the Department of Fredericksburg, Virginia, as a colonel in the Confederate States Army, Pickett was promoted to brigadier general on January 14, 1862. He cut a colorful figure astride his horse, Old Black. Known for his immaculate and well-tailored uniforms, the new general sported gold spurs on his polished boots and always carried a riding crop. Pickett wore a long, drooping mustache, and his hair hung ringlets over his shoulders. He kept his beard meticulously trimmed and was fond of wearing cologne.

Though he appeared to be a dandy, Pickett saw impressive combat at Williamsburg and Seven Pines before being shot off his horse at Gaines' Mill while leading a charge. Though afoot, the general continued to lead his men despite a severe shoulder wound that kept him off the battlefield for three months. He suffered stiffness in the arm for a year after his recuperation.

Returning to the army in September 1862, Pickett was given command of a division consisting of two brigades under his old friend James Longstreet. In October, Pickett became a major general, and his division was upgraded with three additional brigades. Absent for the Confederate victory at the Battle of Chancellorsville, Pickett's name has come to be forever associated with defeat at Gettysburg.

Before his ill-fated charge, Pickett courted his third wife, teenage LaSalle "Sallie" Corbell, whom he married in November 1863. She was nineteen, the groom 38.

Following the debacle of Gettysburg, Picket commanded the Department of Southern Virginia and North Carolina, where he again faced defeat at the Battle of New Bern. Controversially, Pickett ordered the execution of twenty-two captured Union soldiers, all natives of North Carolina loyal to the United States. The youngest of the number was only fifteen.

For the remainder of the war, Pickett assisted with the defense of Richmond, fought in the Battle of Cold Harbor, and participated in the Battle of Five Forks. Some sources maintain that Pickett was relieved of his command in the closing days of the war, though if the orders were issued, they no longer exist. Regardless, Pickett was present at the Battle of Appomattox Courthouse and surrendered with Lee.

After the war, Pickett was haunted by the death of his men at Gettysburg, meeting only once with Lee in an exchange characterized as chilly. When reporters would question Pickett about his defeat on July 3, he often responded that the Yankees "had something to do with it."

When the war ended, Pickett fled to Canada rather than face prosecution for the Union soldier executions, returning only when he received General Grant's personal assurance of his immunity.

Pickett died of a liver abscess in Norfolk, Virginia, on July 30, 1875. Initially buried there, he was removed in October and taken to

Richmond with more than 40,000 mourners lining the route of his casket. Some 5,000 participants marched in the subsequent procession. The memorial to Pickett dedicated in 1888 was not placed over his grave, the location of which remains disputed.

Sallie, who outlived her husband by fifty-five years, dedicated her life to creating a mythic portrait of Pickett. She wrote two books about him that were largely efforts in hagiography, but in the South, the general remains a tragic hero.

Preparing for Pickett's Charge

Selecting his only fresh troops for the assault, Lee committed Pickett's Virginia men to their fate—three brigades from the I Corps—totaling 5,500, including officers. To bolster their numbers, he added two brigades under the command of Maj. Gen. Isaac R. Trimble to Heth's division, now commanded by Pettigrew, for a total of 13,000 men.

Because the attack would take place over almost a mile of open ground, Lee ordered an artillery bombardment ahead of the infantry action. He focused the action on a group of trees near the middle of Cemetery Ridge. Finally, Lee put Longstreet in charge of the attack. To the general's surprise, the commander he referred to as "my old war horse" suggested Hill be put in charge instead, arguing that a third of the forces to be engaged came from the III Corps. After a withering look from Lee, however, Longstreet relented.

When the 1,300 Confederate guns opened fire, many of the shells overshot their target, striking the Union ambulances and supply chains behind Cemetery Ridge. Even Meade's headquarters came under fire and were evacuated after several staff members suffered wounds.

The shells that did strike the mark dismounted guns from their caissons, killing the gunners and draft horses. The Federals fired back, but the chief of artillery General Hunt argued with General Hancock, who wanted a steady barrage to bolster morale. Hunt wanted to conserve ammunition by firing only well-aimed shots. The II Corps gunners obeyed Hancock, exacting a definite toll on Lee's artillery. The shots that went long exploded in the ranks of the infantrymen waiting to begin the attack, killing or mutilating the troops.

Analysts of the battle point to the time distortion effect that often occurs in the heat of fighting. While locals listening to the bombardment at a distance describe minutes of sustained firing, participants estimated shelling that lasted from two to four hours. At one point, the artillery hief for the Confederate I Corps, Lt. Col. E. Porter Alexander, ommunicated with Longstreet, urging the general to start the attack efore the ammunition was spent. But when the guns fell silent, .ongstreet still hesitated. He did not believe the attack would succeed. Vhen Pickett confronted him and asked for the order to begin the idvance, Longstreet responded with a nod only. What happened next las both mythological and realistic elements in the retelling.

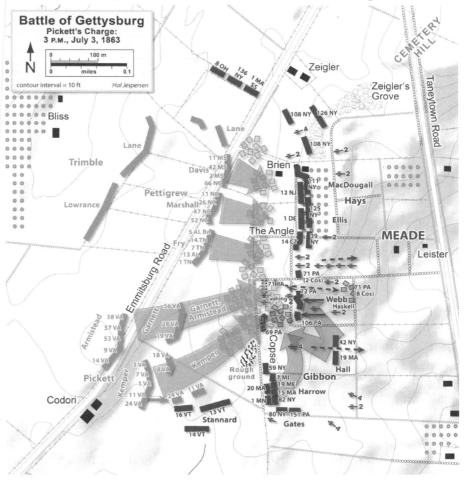

Map of Pickett's Charge.
*Map by Hal Jespersen, www.posix.com/CW, CC BY 3.0
<https://creativecommons.org/licenses/by/3.0>, via Wikimedia Commons;
https://commons.wikimedia.org/wiki/File:Pickett%27s-Charge-detail.png*

Illustrations of Pickett's charge tend to depict parade-ground straight lines emerging from the cover of the trees on Seminary Ridge. This battlefield art gives the impression of an advance over level ground. In truth, Pickett's men waited in the low depressions surrounding the Spangler farm buildings. This put them well behind the trees and to the right center of the Confederate line.

Brigadier generals Richard B. Garnett and James L. Kemper put their brigades in front of the farm structures, while Brig. Gen. Lewis A. Armistead's men were behind Garnett, sheltering behind a low ridge. The troops couldn't see the trees on Cemetery Ridge, and the Federals couldn't see them.

Pettigrew and Trimble were equally protected approximately 600 yards north of Pickett, also behind the trees. Thus, when the attack was ordered, two forces advanced—Pickett from the low ground and Pettigrew and Trimble from the trees on Seminary Ridge.

Pickett ordered a left oblique march to join his men with Pettigrew's line. Until the Confederates reached the halfway point, they suffered only light casualties, but when Pickett's men neared the Emmitsburg Road, Hancock's II Corps artillery and several Union batteries had a clear view of the advance.

The Union gunners switched from shell to canister. These short-range shells loaded with lead balls amounted to giant shotguns aimed at the Confederates. Adding to this deadly effect, the artillerymen fired double canister—two rounds loaded and fired with a single charge. As soon as the 8th Ohio Infantry found their range, they began a heavy musket barrage.

The fact that Pickett and Pettigrew's men found each other at the Emmitsburg Road was more of an accident than deliberate coordination. Their forward movement was broken by post and rail fencing. Once over, Garnett broke to the left, and Kemper swung to the right. In so doing, they passed two Union brigades that later claimed they'd driven the enemy from the area with intense fire.

Pettigrew and Trimble aimed for a section of the line held by Brig. Gen. Alexander Hays's division, positioned behind the rock walls that ran along Cemetery Ridge to the north and south. One wall, however, stood closer to the ridge, connected to the others by a perpendicular section, creating an area known as the Angle. If Pickett's men reached the northern ranks first, they would strike there.

After twenty minutes of crossing open ground, Garnett and Kemper's troops halted before the stone wall and traded shots with their Federal ounterparts. When the Federals appeared to waiver before the Confederate onslaught, Lt. Alonzo H. Cushing, the commander of Battery A, 4th U.S. Artillery, moved his three intact guns forward in support. Wounded and weak, Cushing issued his orders through a subordinate.

When Pickett's boys broke the line in two places, the 1st New York Independent Battery responded with point-blank double canisters, sealing the breaches. Kemper fell wounded and Garnett was killed, leaving Armistead to lead the next Confederate penetration of the northern position. He went through the wall north of the cluster of trees, sending the Union troops reeling. Cushing, having expended his canister, lay dead on the field from a head wound.

Rallying, the Federals drove the Confederates back over the wall, but Armistead suffered a mortal wound and Hancock was severely injured. The Virginians needed reinforcements, but Hill's brigades marched toward the Union guns rather than the original target—the copse of trees. There, canister fire again halted the Confederate advance as Brig. Gen. George J. Stannard's brigade issued blistering fire against Pickett's right flank. After twenty minutes of hard fighting, many of the Virginians surrendered, while others fell back.

On Pickett's left, some of Pettigrew and Trimble's troops made it farther up the slope of Cemetery Ridge, but they could not get past the recessed stone wall where the Federals fired from four massed lines. The first volley caused such death and confusion in the Southern ranks that many of the soldiers threw down their arms and surrendered.

Though both North Carolina and Mississippi units claimed to have reached the farthest point during the doomed Confederate advance, the boasts rang hollow in the face of the slaughter. As the survivors straggled back to Seminary Ridge, General Lee met them astride his horse, Traveler, saying, "It's all my fault." At the same time, however, he expected Pickett to rally and try again. Stunned at the 60 percent casualty rate, Pickett told Lee he no longer had a division to field.

As the Confederate action raged, General Jeb Stuart, who arrived on July 2, skirmished with Union cavalry four miles east of town. Although Lee would have little to say about his errant general, Stuart maintained that his actions that day ensured complete security on Ewell's left and put him in place to disrupt the Union retreat—which never happened.

Dismounted troops in Union Brig. Gen. David M. Gregg's division fired on the Southerners near the Rummel farm. In the intense fighting, Confederate Brig. Gen. Wade Hampton's cavalrymen charged across the open fields near the Hanover Road, sabers drawn, with Brig. Gen. George Armstrong Custer's Michigan cavalry on an intercept course. The Union troops broke the charge, one of the greatest of the war.

At the same time, Union troops assaulted the Confederate right flank to the southwest. The actions harassed the enemy and forced some troop relocations but were largely unsuccessful. Union Brig. Gen. Elon J. Farnsworth fell during a futile cavalry charge repulsed by the Southerners to savage effect. Farnsworth was the last general officer to die in action at Gettysburg, and the charge ended the fighting on July 3.

Saturday, July 4, 1863

As July 4 dawned, the two armies remained on the battlefield, but only the occasional shot disrupted the eerie calm that had descended over the countryside. Meade congratulated his troops and directed the burial of Confederate dead lying within Union lines. By noon, the heat and intense humidity sparked thunderstorms. The rain brought on flash flooding by evening, with many severely wounded men drowning where they had fallen.

During the night, the Confederate II Corps had withdrawn from Culp's Hill to consolidate with Lee's remaining force on Seminary Ridge. When Union skirmishers ventured into Gettysburg on July 5, they found the town devoid of Confederate troops. The Southerners had begun the long march back to Virginia in defeat.

Lee ordered his infantry and artillery to make for the Potomac River crossings at Williamsport and Falling Waters. They took approximately 5,000 Union prisoners with them under the watch of Pickett's surviving troops. The Southern wounded were loaded in wagons and taken south along the Chambersburg Pike in a seventeen-mile-long caravan protected by a brigade of cavalry commanded by Brig. Gen. John D. Imboden.

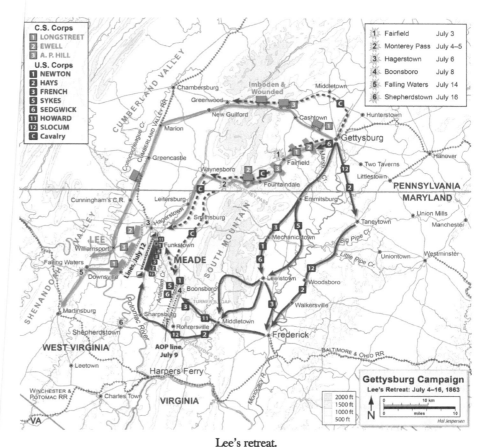

Lee's retreat.

*Map by Hal Jespersen, www.cwmaps.com, CC BY 3.0
<https://creativecommons.org/licenses/by/3.0>, via Wikimedia Commons;
https://commons.wikimedia.org/wiki/File:Gettysburg_Campaign_Retreat.png*

Meade sent cavalry to disrupt Lee's retreat on July 4, striking the wagon trains, liberating Union soldiers, and taking the wounded captive. The next day, Meade sent the VI Corps under Maj. Gen. John Sedgwick along the Fairfield Road, but the general stopped when the Confederates turned and fought. Because the Southerners were moving through narrow breaks in the mountains, Sedgwick concluded the terrain favored his enemy. Meade agreed and gave up the idea of pursuing the Army of Northern Virginia, intending instead to thwart Lee's efforts to cross the Potomac.

Meade allowed Lee to move well ahead of the Union Army, but when the Confederates arrived at Williamsport on July 10, they discovered Union cavalry had destroyed the pontoon bridge at Falling

Waters. Additionally, heavy rains had caused the river to flood. Lee had no choice but to dig in behind fortifications erected by his exhausted men while engineers rebuilt the bridge.

When Meade arrived at Williamsport on July 12, he found Lee's army waiting behind earthworks in a formidable line. Still, Meade wanted to attack, but his corps commanders counseled caution. Meade decided to wait, hoping for better weather. The next day, Lee's engineers finished the bridge. Under a driving rain, the Army of Northern Virginia reached the far shore of the Potomac. On the morning of the 14th, the Federals found themselves facing an empty position. Buford briefly skirmished at Falling Waters with Lee's rearguard, an engagement that resulted in the mortal wounding of Confederate General Pettigrew. Otherwise, Lee successfully retreated to the relative safety of Virginia.

Lincoln, buoyed by Grant's victory at Vicksburg, had hoped to see the war wrapped up with a decisive blow against the defeated Lee. When that didn't happen, the president vented his frustration, saying that no matter what he said or did, his army would not move. Lincoln did not grasp, however, that though victorious, the Army of the Potomac was almost as battered as that of Northern Virginia. The Union ranks had suffered heavy losses among the officer corps and the rank and file. The men were hungry, and many marched barefoot, their shoes worn out on the paved roads of Pennsylvania or lost to the sucking mud in Maryland.

Had reinforcements been dispatched from Washington, Meade might have been able to take more aggressive action, but no help was forthcoming. The Gettysburg campaign left both armies in tattered condition, with no end to the war in sight. Though beaten on the field at Gettysburg, the Confederates were not done and would indeed fight on for almost two more years.

Chapter 6 – Citizens, Doctors, Photographers, Posterity

Often absent in battlefield accounts of Gettysburg are considerations of how the town's citizens participated in or were affected by the events of those three days. They were not strangers to the threat of Confederate forces nearby. The town, then comprised of 2,400 residents, lies only ten miles north of the Mason-Dixon Line. Freed people in the area were often subject to kidnappings, and Southern troops conducted small-scale raiding actions into Pennsylvania. Though rumors had circulated of an invasion since the beginning of the war, those fears were realized in late June and early July 1863.

The epic battle transformed the lives and the landscape of Gettysburg, but the experiences of the residents ranged from tragic to heroic, with the occasional hint of macabre humor.

The morning of July 1 found Pennsylvania College student Robert McClean in class with professor of mathematics Dr. Michael Jacobs (who became one of the first authors to pen an account of the battle within months of its conclusion). To the professor's frustration, the sound of gunfire and artillery distracted his students so thoroughly that he gave in and dismissed the class. Anxious to see what was happening, McClean set out for Seminary Ridge only to have a cannon shot pass directly overhead. Later, McClean candidly admitted that the experience greatly improved his relationship with the Scriptures.

Sophia Culp Epley, a housewife and mother, had more immediate concerns than two battling armies. She found a gang of Confederates trying to make off with her cow. Yelling at the top of her lungs, she drove the interlopers away, oblivious to any personal danger. After all, Epley needed the milk for her children.

At the south end of Baltimore Street, John and Caroline Rupp lived with their six children near the base of Cemetery Hill. The home and adjacent tannery lay smack between the Union and Confederate lines. Correctly reading the danger, Rupp sent his family first to the neighbors and then to his father's home. Reluctant to leave his property, John Rupp hid in his basement for the rest of the battle while Confederate and Union snipers, oblivious to each other's presence, used the building as their base.

Catherine Garlach, on the other hand, directly faced the Confederate sniper who wanted to set up in her home. She lectured the man, chiding him for endangering innocents, until he hung his head in shame and left—without firing a shot.

Many residents kept journals during the fighting. Some, like Sallie Broadhead, confessed that the exercise was as much about relieving anxiety as creating a historical record. Though valuable for their insight into civilians caught in the thick of war, many such accounts are wholly inaccurate in their recollection of troop movements.

Still, the journals convey the writers' shocked disbelief that war had finally come to their doorstep, the fear and confusion of being caught between the armies, and the incredible relief when the whole thing was over. These sources and the stories published in the town's two weekly newspapers, *The Star and Sentinel* and *The Compiler*, collected eyewitness reports into the early 1900s that would have otherwise been lost.

Without them, we could not look through the eyes of Gates Fahnestock, a ten-year-old boy who peeked through the shutters of his home as Jubal Early's men rode through town firing their guns, officer's swords held high. To the child, the whole thing looked like "a Wild West show." At the same time, Sarah Barrett King could not help but note the ragged, filthy condition of the invaders, many of whom marched without shoes.

Perhaps Jennie McCreary put the town's stunned reaction best when she wrote to her sister, "We never expected a battle." But the battle rrived all the same, putting residents in the crosshairs. Some, like Jennie Wade, would simply be at the wrong place at the wrong time. In Jennie's case, she became the only local to die in the battle.

Jennie Wade

Wade, a Gettysburg native, worked with her mother as a seamstress. She had a sister and two younger brothers. The absent father resided in a mental institute. Born on May 21, 1843, Jennie was only twenty when she became an accidental casualty of war, felled by a stray bullet on July 3.

Ironically, on the first day of the battle, Jennie, her mother, and siblings were at the home of Georgia Anna Wade McClellan on Baltimore Street to help care for Georgia's newborn child. An estimated 150 bullets struck the building while they were there.

On Friday, July 3, 1863, still at her sister's house, Jennie was in the kitchen making bread. A Minié ball came through the door and struck Jennie in the back, passing through her left shoulder blade and striking her heart. She died instantly. The source of the shot has never been confirmed but is typically attributed to a Confederate sniper.

Mrs. Wade heard her daughter's body hit the floor. Two Union soldiers present in the house came downstairs when they heard screaming. The men buried Wade in the backyard; they used a coffin meant for General William Barksdale, mortally wounded after leading a charge on horseback through the Peach Orchard near Plum Run. He died on the morning of July 3.

Jennie's body was exhumed in January 1864 and buried in the graveyard of the German Reformed Church on Stratton Street. Since November 1865, she has rested in Gettysburg's Evergreen Cemetery. An American flag flies over her grave twenty-four hours a day; she's the only woman other than Betsy Ross to have been given this honor.

John Lawrence Burns

When Confederate General Jubal Early occupied Gettysburg briefly on June 26, 1863, his soldiers met the implacable will of Constable John Lawrence Burns, sixty-nine, a veteran of the War of 1812. He protested the Southern presence with such vehemence that the troops put him in a jail cell rather than deal with him. Released upon their departure, Burns, undeterred, gave chase and arrested a handful of stragglers.

On July 1, 1863, still determined to oppose the invasion, Burns walked toward the sound of the guns with a flintlock musket in hand. Before he reached the thick of the fighting, he talked a wounded Federal soldier out of his Enfield rifle and cartridges. Armed and ready for action, Burns asked Maj. Thomas Chamberlin for permission to fight alongside the 150th Pennsylvania Infantry.

Chamberlin later described Burns as wearing dark pants and a matching waistcoat under a blue coat with brass buttons and sporting a well-worn top hat. Uncertain about what to do with the unlikely volunteer, Chamberlin sent Burns to Colonel Langhorne Wister, the regimental commander, who sent the old man into McPherson Woods.

There, Burns fought with the 7th Wisconsin before joining the 24th Michigan, or Iron Brigade, staying with them and functioning as a sharpshooter for the afternoon. Burns exhibited superior marksmanship, even knocking a charging Confederate officer from the saddle.

As the Union line broke, however, the Federals had no choice but to leave their new compatriot behind. Burns had been wounded in the arm and ankle, with minor injuries to his chest. Ever resourceful, Burns laid down his rifle, crawled some distance, and buried his ammunition.

When discovered by Confederate troops, he played the part of an innocent civilian who had ventured to the battlefield hoping to find a medic to treat his sick wife. The Southerners dressed his wounds, and later Burns made it to the cellar of a nearby house and ultimately home.

In the aftermath of the battle, Burns's story made him a national hero. After Lincoln delivered the Gettysburg Address on November 19, 1863, the president made time for a walk with the elderly combatant.

Burns lived ten years after the battle but suffered from dementia for the last two years of his life. Given to wandering, he reached New York City in December 1871, where he was found freezing and destitute on the streets. Burns was given medical attention and sent home, succumbing to pneumonia on February 4, 1872.

A statue commemorating Burns's participation in the battle sits atop a boulder on McPherson's Ridge. Dedicated forty years after his actions on July 1, 1903, the sculpture depicts Burns with a defiant air, rifle clutched in one hand, the other balled into a fist. The old man rests in Evergreen Cemetery, and, like Jennie Wade, his grave is marked by a perpetual American flag. His marker bears the simple epitaph "Patriot."

Elizabeth Salome "Sallie" Myers

Like many women in Gettysburg, schoolteacher Elizabeth Salome Myers nursed the sick and wounded—Federal and Confederate—despite her later admission that she couldn't bear the sight of blood. When the surgeon of the 143rd Pennsylvania Volunteers, Dr. James Fulton, put out a call for nurses, Myers answered, only to flee the hospital set up at St. Francis Catholic Church when her first patient declined her offer of help, saying he was dying.

Quick to recover from her shock, however, Myers went back to the bedside of the same patient, Sergeant Alexander Stewart, who wanted to hear the fourteenth chapter of the book of John. He explained that his family read the passage aloud before he and his brother left for the war. Soothing the dying man's last minutes strengthened her resolve. Myers continued working as a nurse throughout the summer. On the fortieth anniversary of the battle, she published *How a Gettysburg Schoolteacher Spent Her Vacation in 1863.*

Field Hospitals

As the battle raged, field medical stations were set up, sometimes less than 100 yards from the fighting. These stations had to be ready to move with little-to-no notice as the fighting drew closer. Marked by a red hospital flag, they served to apply rudimentary dressings before directing the wounded to hospitals where they could receive more care. In the extreme heat of the first three days of July and the torrential rains that followed, overtaxed doctors provided what care they could.

Doctors used lint to pack wounds and splints to stabilize broken bones. Tourniquets and pressure dressings were applied only as temporary measures for men in immediate need of surgery. Soldiers with bowel or chest wounds were given pain relief, usually opium. Partially severed fingers were amputated immediately.

As soon as these doctors could do so, they left the fighting and reported to field hospitals, where they worked all night by candlelight. The field hospitals used by the Army of the Potomac medical department included the following:

- I Corps, Lutheran Theological Seminary (July 1), White Church on the Baltimore Pike (July 2)

- II Corps – adjacent to Rock Creek east of the Bushman House (July 2)

- III Corps – Taneytown Road, White Run, and Rock Creek (July 2)
- V Corps – Taneytown Road west of Round Top (July 2), Two Taverns (July 3)
- VI Corps – Trostle House
- XI Corps – Spangler House
- XII Corps – Bushman House
- Cavalry Corps – Presbyterian Church and other buildings in Gettysburg

The wounded either straggled into these makeshift facilities of their own accord or were taken by ambulance. All bore the hideous wounds of modern warfare. Their bones shattered by exploding artillery and flesh rent by canister shot and bullets, many looked barely human.

Bloody, bruised, and in agony, they found themselves at the mercy of medical science that had not yet embraced the rudiments of germ theory. The knives and saws used by the doctors were, at most, dipped in buckets of bloody water between procedures.

Men who were gut shot or had suffered head wounds often had the greatest chance of surviving because the doctors considered them lost causes. Though in excruciating pain, the abdominal cases were at least spared the danger of infection inherent in the surgeries of the day. Gangrene killed as many soldiers as bullets. The survivors of head wounds, dazed and confused, were confined in pens to keep them from wandering off. A good percentage of those cases lived, though often suffering the symptoms of a traumatic brain injury for life.

With approximately 30,000 Union and Confederate patients needing medical attention, the field hospitals in and around Gettysburg operated into August 1863. On the first day of the battle, the casualty total had already reached 16,000. Many of these men were taken to a hospital set up in the McPherson barn. The adjacent farmhouse had been in the thick of the battle all day. Control of the property passed back and forth between the warring armies. Riddled with bullets, the building still provided shelter for the wounded and dying. There, Union and Confederate doctors worked side by side in blood-splattered aprons.

More of the wounded were taken to the barn, where surgeons labored to dress wounds and perform amputations. Thirst and hunger exacerbated the suffering of the soldiers. Some waited so long to get help they had to be pulled free of the congealed blood holding them fast to the floorboards.

Alerted to the suffering, Gettysburg residents prepared food and water, which they brought to the barn despite their natural fear of coming so close to the battlefront. William McClean, headed toward the McPherson Farm with biscuits, gruel, and fresh raspberries, passed burial parties interring soldiers where they had fallen while artillery fired in the distance.

(The work of burying the dead began immediately on the first day. With so many corpses lying on the field, the fear of contagion was real and serious. Burial parties hastily dug shallow graves. The dead, if identifiable, were recognized by penciled names on wooden boards as makeshift markers.)

Meanwhile, at Pennsylvania College on July 1, Confederate Chief Surgeon Samuel B. Morrison ordered that the buildings be used as field hospitals, including the home of college president Henry Baugher, whose wife (Clarissa) and daughter (Alice) worked as nurses. The Baughers' only son had died a year earlier at the Battle of Shiloh, which inspired the family to stay and help even as shells exploded around them.

One of the Confederates to be treated in Pennsylvania Hall was Colonel Waller Tazewell Patton of the 7th Virginia, whose great-nephew would be General George S. Patton of World War II fame. An artillery shell blew off Colonel Patton's lower jaw during Pickett's charge on July 3. The wound made breathing difficult, forcing the injured man to sit upright, leaning against a wall. When he became too weak to hold himself up, volunteer nurse Euphemia "Miss Effie" Goldsborough held him in place with the weight of her own body. Astonishingly and painfully, the colonel lived until July 21.

The level of dedication shown by Goldsborough was not the exception among these gallant medical professionals but rather the rule. When the battle was lost, Confederate Dr. Lewis E. Gott of the 49th Virginia Infantry and several of his colleagues refused to abandon their patients. The doctors stayed behind, working with the Union medical staff until they were sent to Fort McHenry in Baltimore as prisoners of war.

Pennsylvania Hall was used as a hospital until July 29, but the marks of its service lingered long after the last wounded man left the premises. For years, the floors remained stained with blood, as did many of the books used as headrests for the wounded. A number of those books now reside in the Musselman Library's Gettysburg College Special Collections.

In 1937, during excavations around the north portico of the building, workers unearthed bits of bone. It was common for surgeons to toss amputated limbs into piles—usually out a window or door—to be buried later.

Among the numerous sites in and around the battlefield considered to be haunted, Pennsylvania Hall has been the site of numerous encounters with the paranormal. Students report objects that move independently and sightings of a solitary soldier who circles the school's cupola late at night.

In the wake of the battle, Union leaders quickly realized that this network of makeshift hospitals, which had then expanded to some sixty sites, could not handle the incredible volume of recuperating men. While many were transported to Baltimore or Philadelphia, others were housed in what became, for a time, the largest field hospital in the Western Hemisphere.

Construction began on July 8 on eighty acres belonging to George Wolf a mile northeast of Gettysburg on the York Pike. The area was chosen for its proximity to the railroad, location on high ground, ample shade, and fresh spring water. Named for the medical director of the Army of the Potomac, Dr. Jonathan Letterman, the camp opened on July 22 and operated until January 1864. There, approximately 100 doctors treated more than 21,000 soldiers with only 1,200 deaths, a remarkable accomplishment for the time.

Patients were housed in more than 400 tents spaced at ten feet. Each could hold a dozen patients, with each doctor in charge of forty-seven men. Camp Letterman was, for all purposes, a small city, with separate quarters for officers and staff, an administrative building, a store run by the United States Christian Commission volunteers, and a delegation from the U.S. Sanitary Commission.

There were also funerary facilities for embalming and a nearby cemetery. Later, many of the Confederate dead were relocated to the South, while the Union soldiers were moved to the national cemetery.

Today, the site is a shopping center off the Lincoln Highway.

Battlefield Photography

Many casual students of history believe that one of America's pioneering photographers, Mathew Brady, personally photographed the aftermath of the Gettysburg battlefield. In fact, Brady's eyesight had begun to deteriorate by the 1850s. He did, however, shoot thousands of portraits of young soldiers in his New York studio. Both an artist and a businessman, Brady posted ads in regional newspapers urging parents to secure photographs of their sons in case they were killed at war. To chronicle the fighting, Brady hired field assistants.

Brady was born to Irish immigrants in Warren County, New York, in either 1822 or 1824. Initially, he studied painting but switched to the emerging field of photography, which thoroughly captured his imagination.

Brady studied technique with Samuel Morse, who learned the daguerreotype method from Louis Jacques Daguerre in France in 1839. During the Civil War, however, the most popular method was albumen silver, which produced a paper photograph from a large glass negative.

Though his portraits of departing soldiers were popular and profitable, Brady yearned to capture the gritty reality of war itself. He first petitioned his friend General Winfield Scott for permission to work on the nation's battlefields, but the approval came from President Lincoln in 1861—with the caveat that Brady be self-financed.

At this early stage, Brady did travel to the front. He got so close to the fighting at the First Battle of Bull Run (July 21) he was very nearly captured. After that, and assessing the massive scope of the task at hand, Brady outfitted twenty-three assistants with mobile studios and dark rooms. For the remainder of the year, he directed their efforts at a distance from his New York studio.

In October 1862, Brady mounted an exhibition entitled "The Dead of Antietam," which brought the brutality of war home to the American public for the first time. In all previous wars, only eyewitnesses had seen the carnage of the battlefield. Now, average citizens were forced to confront the real cost of the conflict.

The images that most shocked the nation, however, were those taken by Timothy O'Sullivan, an Irishman who had begun working for Brady while still a teenager. O'Sullivan, along with Alexander Gardner and James Gibson, captured the horrors of Gettysburg for posterity.

O'Sullivan's most famous image, "A Harvest of Death," shows the rotting dead of Gettysburg lying where they had fallen, awaiting burial. That single photograph, however, was but a fraction of the pictures O'Sullivan shot in July 1863. In one vivid still after another, he captured the broken bodies of fallen soldiers, bloated in death, their limbs twisted at odd angles, lifeless hands reaching for help that never arrived.

Through his lens, Americans saw the ghastly wounds caused by artillery, counted the bodies of fallen soldiers lying limply over the boulders of Devil's Den, and beheld dead snipers resting beside their now silent rifles. O'Sullivan captured the grim jobs of burial parties and the brutal work of doctors in field hospitals. So acute was Sullivan's eye for the battlefield's salient landmarks that those photographs can be exactly matched with the same locations today in chilling "then and now" comparisons.

Action shots were not possible, as 19th-century cameras required the subjects to stand still, but something about the frozen quality of the surviving pictures make them even more poignant.

Though it fell from favor with the war-weary public after the fighting was over, Brady's body of work, paired with the efforts of his men in the field, constitutes one of the most visceral and compelling records of the American Civil War. Because of Brady, we have excellent portraits of generals from both armies, Abraham Lincoln, Jefferson Davis, and other significant political leaders. All are priceless national treasures.

Preserving the Battlefield

Four and a half months after the last shot was fired at Gettysburg, on the afternoon of November 19, 1863, President Abraham Lincoln delivered the sparse and well-crafted Gettysburg Address. He was not, however, the featured speaker at the Consecration of the Soldiers' National Cemetery at Gettysburg. That honor went to Reverend Edward Everett, a Unitarian minister from Massachusetts known for his work in education, diplomacy, and politics. The former secretary of state (for Millard Fillmore), congressman (in both the Senate and House), governor, and U.S. minister to the United Kingdom composed an oration of 13,607 words. He spoke for two hours, and no one remembers what he said.

Lincoln jotted down at least five drafts of his remarks—none on the back of an envelope, as legend would have us believe—and every version, including those reprinted in newspapers, is different. We don't even know exactly where the platform stood from which the president delivered his thoughts. Yet almost every American can quote all or some of Lincoln's Gettysburg Address.

The occasion was the reburial of Union soldiers taken from scattered graves across the countryside to the new Gettysburg National Cemetery. Less than half of that work, which began on October 17, had been completed.

Few knew that Lincoln was ill that day, complaining of nausea, dizziness, fever, and a headache. When he returned to Washington, D.C., on the 6:30 p.m. train, the president subsequently developed a rash characterized by blisters that led to a diagnosis of mild smallpox.

But regardless of his position on the day's program or his physical condition, Lincoln hit a note in his speech that resonated with Americans. When he said, "These dead shall not have died in vain," he touched a national chord that still sounds in Gettysburg today.

Residents of the Pennsylvania town, now surrounded by the Gettysburg National Military Park, readily admit they feel the presence of the men who died there in 1863. Every year, they celebrate the anniversary of Lincoln's speech on Remembrance Day, an occasion marked by a parade and the presence of thousands of Civil War re-enactors.

Others admit to seeing ghostly regiments in the dim light of dusk and dawn or phantom horsemen galloping across the silent fields. Tourist photos sometimes inexplicably show faces and figures not present when the shutter clicked. Though we might scoff at these ghost stories, Union troops on the battlefield in July 1863 swore they saw the ghost of George Washington leading them to victory.

Gettysburg is unquestionably a place where the dead play a role in everyday life. The national cemetery holds the graves of 3,512 combatants—979 unknown. There are also sections for the dead of the Spanish-American War (1898) and World War I (for American involvement, 1917-1918). The graves number more than 6,000. In the center of the site stands a sixty-foot granite monument, the work of sculptor Randolph Rogers and architect George Keller. Concentric half-circles of the Gettysburg dead grouped by state flank the memorial.

In the larger Gettysburg National Military Park, a site where the National Park Service is tasked with protecting and interpreting the battlefield, visitors can tour the areas where the fighting occurred, as well as those associated with supporting functions (field hospitals) and the aftermath. The adjacent museum and visitors center houses more than 43,000 artifacts. More are found each year.

Preservation of the site began as early as 1864 when the Gettysburg Battlefield Memorial Association was formed. Along with veterans' groups after the war, the Association acquired land and took up collections to create various memorials that now dot the landscape. In 1893, the federal government began purchasing these acquisitions. The future park was established by an act of Congress on February 11, 1895, under the direction of the secretary of war. Four other Civil War battlefields are maintained as parks, including Vicksburg, Shiloh, Chickamauga/Chattanooga, and Antietam.

The work of the park service at Gettysburg is ongoing, with efforts to restore the battlefield to its 1863 condition by thinning wooded areas absent in the 19th century and replanting key orchards and fields. Neither the men who died there nor the landscape on which they lost their lives is neglected, for, as Lincoln said, "The world will little note, nor long remember what we say here, but it can never forget what they did here."

Conclusion

Initially, the victory at Gettysburg on the heels of Vicksburg touched off a wave of euphoric celebration in the North. Only slowly did the public come to understand that the end of the war was not in sight. Lincoln expressed bitter disappointment in Meade's failure to definitively crush Lee.

The Army of the Potomac suffered immense loss during the Gettysburg campaign: 3,155 killed in action, 14,529 wounded. Two thousand of these died in the following weeks. Including the 5,365 missing, the number of casualties reached 23,049, or roughly a quarter of the Northern soldiers who participated in the battle.

Though criticized, Meade had fulfilled his orders. He protected Washington, D.C., and Baltimore and engaged Lee in battle. He also forced an invading army out of Union territory, capturing three large guns, the standards of forty-one units, small arms totaling 24,978 weapons, and taking 13,621 prisoners.

As a battlefield commander, Meade effectively used interior lines to support his troops in scattered positions in and around Gettysburg. He utilized the manpower at his disposal and sought the consensus of his subordinates before acting. In so doing, he cost the Army of Northern Virginia 20,451 casualties: 2,592 dead, 12,709 wounded, and 5,150 missing, equaling a third of Lee's troops.

Holding himself responsible for the defeat of his troops, Lee offered his resignation to Confederate President Jefferson Davis, but without success. Almost from the moment the Gettysburg Campaign ended, blame was apportioned, but less fell on Lee than his subordinates.

Newspapers in the south pointed to Jeb Stuart's long absence and criticized Ewell for failing to take Cemetery Hill. Editors alleged that General Richard Anderson hadn't committed sufficient troops to the action on July 2 and that Pettigrew hadn't effectively supported Pickett. Interestingly, Longstreet emerged largely unscathed in the court of public opinion. This is ironic since, in the post-war years, he was thoroughly condemned for his perceived failures at Gettysburg to the point of being made a scapegoat.

The campaign—and, most specifically, the July 1–July 3, 1863 battle—retains a mythic importance when examined in the context of the overall war. Gettysburg is now regarded as the turning point in the conflict, the beginning of the end for the Confederacy, though that end would be long and bloody in coming.

This examination has attempted to convey the major movement of troops from late June 1863 when Lee decided to cross into Pennsylvania until his retreat in early July. No work of this length can definitively dissect the Battle of Gettysburg, however, as the extensive bibliography that follows will show.

Gettysburg remains one of the most heavily studied confrontations of the American Civil War. There is a body of scholarship replete with unit histories and the evaluation of officers and their decisions up and down the chain of command on both sides. There are excellent biographies of all the major participants and many of the lesser-known but equally valiant combatants.

Armchair generals continue to ponder how different decisions at pivotal moments might have changed the outcome, pushing miniature soldiers around tabletop reconstructions or probing potential outcomes in realistic video simulations.

The Battle of Gettysburg has a way of getting into people's blood, compelling them to dig deeper, look back over the years, and truly understand what happened on the fields and craggy outcroppings of Pennsylvania. For many students, the battle becomes a lifelong obsession.

Lee, in his usual stoic manner, wrote to his wife on July 12, 1863, telling her that before she received his letter, she would learn that "...our success at Gettysburg was not so great as reported..." Astonishingly, in his correspondence with President Jefferson Davis, Lee's optimism appeared undaunted. He told Davis that reversals and defeats were to be expected in war and could be viewed as lessons in prudence and wisdom. Defeat, according to Lee, encouraged men to try harder, to learn from their mistakes, and to keep them from falling into even larger disasters. What mattered was the united nature of the Southern people who, through their forbearance of misfortune, would see all "come right in the end."

Though Lee could not see—or perhaps refused to see—the coming of the end for the Confederacy, the road to that end began at Gettysburg in a defeat from which the General and the Southern cause never recovered.

Here's another book by Captivating History that you might like

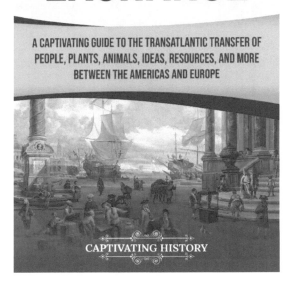

Free Bonus from Captivating History (Available for a Limited time)

Hi History Lovers!

Now you have a chance to join our exclusive history list so you can get your first history ebook for free as well as discounts and a potential to get more history books for free! Simply visit the link below to join.

Captivatinghistory.com/ebook

Also, make sure to follow us on Facebook, Twitter and Youtube by searching for Captivating History.

Selected Bibliography

Adkin, Mark. *The Gettysburg Companion: The Complete Guide to America's Most Famous Battle.* Harrisburg, Pennsylvania: Stackpole Books, 2008.

Albright, Harry. *Gettysburg: Crisis of Command.* Hippocrene Books, 1991.

Archer, John M. *Culp's Hill at Gettysburg: The Mountain Trembled.* Gettysburg, Pennsylvania: Thomas Publications, 2002.

Backus, Paige Gibbons. "Camp Letterman at Gettysburg," 6 December 2021, Battlefields.org.

Barthel, Thomas. *Abner Doubleday – A Civil War Biography.* Jefferson, North Carolina: McFarland & Company, 2010.

Bates, Samuel P. *The Battle of Gettysburg.* Philadelphia, Pennsylvania: T. H. Darrs & Co., 1875.

Beattie, Dan. *Brandy Station 1863: First Step Towards Gettysburg.* United Kingdom: Osprey Publishing, 2009.

Bennett, Gerald R. *Days of "Uncertainty and Dread": The Ordeal Endured by the Citizens of Gettysburg.* Littlestown, Pennsylvania: 1994.

Blair, Jayne E. *The Essential Civil War: A Handbook to the Battles, Armies, Navies and Commanders.* Jefferson, North Carolina: McFarland & Company, Inc., 2006.

Bledsoe, Andrew S. *Citizen-Officers: The Union and Confederate Volunteer Junior Officer Corps in the American Civil War.* Baton Rouge, Louisiana: Louisiana State University Press, 2015.

Bloom, Robert L. *We Never Expected a Battle: The Ordeal Endured by the Citizens at Gettysburg.* Littlestown, Pennsylvania: 1988.

Bonekemper, III, Edward H. *McClellan and Failure: A Study of Civil War Fear, Incompetence and Worse.* Jefferson, North Carolina: McFarland & Company, Inc., 2010.

Bowden, Scott and Bill Ward. *Last Chance for Victory: Robert E. Lee and the Gettysburg Campaign.* New York: Savas Beatie, 2001.

Brown, Kent Masterson. *Retreat from Gettysburg: Lee, Logistics, and the Pennsylvania Campaign.* Chapel Hill: University of North Carolina Press, 2005.

Busey, Travis W. and John W. Busey. *Union Casualties at Gettysburg: A Comprehensive Record.* Jefferson, North Carolina: McFarland & Co., 2011.

Carpenter, John A. *Sword and Olive Branch: Oliver Otis Howard.* Fordham University Press, 1999.

Casdorph, Paul D. *Lee and Jackson.* New York: Paragon House, 1992.

_____. *Confederate General R. S. Ewell: Robert E. Lee's Hesitant Commander.* University Press of Kentucky, 2004.

Catton, Bruce. *Gettysburg: The Final Fury.* New York: Random House, 1974.

Chamberlain, Joshua Lawrence. *Bayonet! Forward: My Civil War Reminiscences.* Stan Clark Military Books, 2003.

Coco, Gregory A. *A Vast Sea of Misery: A History and Guide to the Union and Confederate Field Hospitals at Gettysburg, July 1-November 20, 1863.* Gettysburg, PA: Thomas Publications, 1988.

_____. *A Strange and Blighted Land – Gettysburg: The Aftermath of a Battle.* Gettysburg, Pennsylvania: Thomas Publications, 1995.

_____. *Gettysburg's Confederate Dead.* Gettysburg, Pennsylvania: Thomas Publications, 2003.

Coddington, Edwin B. *The Gettysburg Campaign: A Study in Command.* New York: Scribner's, 1968.

Cooling, Benjamin Franklin. *Jubal Early: Robert E. Lee's "Bad Old Man."* Rowman & Littlefield, 2014.

Crain, Caleb. "How Soon It May Be Too Late." *The New York Times,* 4 August 2013.

Creighton, Margaret S. *The Colors of Courage: Gettysburg's Forgotten History.* New York: Basic Books, 2005.

Dorwart, Dr. Bonnie Brice. "Civil War Hospitals," *Essential Civil War Curriculum.* Essentialcivilwarcurriculum.com.

Dreese, Michael A. *The Hospital on Seminary Ridge and the Battle of Gettysburg.* Jefferson, North Carolina: McFarland & Company, Inc., 2002.

Eicher, David J. *The Longest Night: A Military History of the Civil War.* New York: Simon & Schuster, 2001.

Freeman, Douglas S., *R. E. Lee, A Biography*, four volumes. New York: Charles Scribner's Sons, 1934.

Gallagher, Gary W., ed. *The First Day at Gettysburg: Essays on Confederate and Union Leadership*. Kent, Ohio: Kent State University Press, 1992.

Gindlesperger, James. *Bullets and Bandages: The Aid Stations and Field Hospitals at Gettysburg*. Blair, 2020.

Gordon, Lesley J. *General George E. Pickett in Life and Legend*. Chapel Hill, North Carolina: University of North Carolina Press, 1998.

Gottfried, Bradley M. *The Maps of Gettysburg*. New York: Savas Beatie, 2010.

Gragg, Rod. *The Illustrated Gettysburg Reader: An Eyewitness History of the Civil War's Greatest Battle*. New York: Regnary House, 2013.

Guelzo, Allen C. *Robert E. Lee: A Life*. New York: Penguin Random House, 2022.

Hagan, Neil and Stephen Hyslop. *Atlas of the Civil War: A Comprehensive Guide to the Tactics and Terrain of Battle*. National Geographic, 2009.

Hebert, Walter H. *Fighting Joe Hooker*. Old Soldier Books, 1987.

Hessler, James A. *Sickles at Gettysburg: The Controversial Civil War General Who Committed Murder, Abandoned Little Round Top, and Declared Himself the Hero of Gettysburg*. Savas Beatie, LLC, 2010.

_____ and Britt C. Isenberg. *Gettysburg's Peach Orchard: Longstreet, Sickles, and the Bloody Fight for the "Commanding Ground" Along the Emmitsburg Road*. Savas Beatie, 2019.

Hood, Stephen M. *John Bell Hood: The Rise, Fall, and Resurrection of a Confederate General*. Savas Beatie, LLC, 2013.

Horan, James D. *Timothy O'Sullivan, America's Forgotten Photographer*. Garden City, New York: Doubleday & Company, 1966.

Hunt, Jeffrey W. *Meade and Lee After Gettysburg: The Forgotten Final Stage of the Gettysburg Campaign, from Falling Waters to Culpeper Court House, July 14-31, 1863*. Savas Beatie, 2017.

Jordan, David M. *Winfield Scott Hancock: A Soldier's Life*. Bloomington: Indiana University Press, 1988.

Jorgenson, Jay. *Gettysburg's Bloody Wheatfield*. Shippensburg, Pennsylvania: White Mane Books, 2002.

Kernek, Clyde B. *Field Surgeon at Gettysburg*. Indianapolis: Guild Press of Indiana, 1998.

LaFantasie, Glenn. W. *Twilight at Little Round Top: July 2, 1863 – The Tide Turns at Gettysburg*. Hoboken, New Jersey: John Wiley & Sons, Inc., 2005.

Longacre, Edward G. *General John Buford: A Military Biography*. Conshohocken, Pennsylvania: Combined Books, 1995

Luvaas, Jay, and Harold W. Nelson. *The U.S. Army War College Guide to the Battle of Gettysburg*. 1986.

Mackowski, Chris, Kristopher D. White, and Daniel T. Davis. *Don't Give an Inch: The Second Day at Gettysburg, July 2, 1863 – From Little Round Top to Cemetery Ridge*. El Dorado Hills, California: Savas Beatie, 2016.

Mosby, John S. *Stuart's Cavalry in the Gettysburg Campaign*. New York: Moffat, Yard & Co., 1908.

Nelson, A. H. *The Battles of Chancellorsville and Gettysburg*. Minneapolis, Minnesota: no publisher listed, 1899.

Nesbitt, Mark. *Saber & Scapegoat: J.E.B. Stuart and the Gettysburg Controversy*. Mechanicsburg, Pennsylvania: Stackpole Books, 1994.

Nevins, James H. and William B. Styple. *What Death More Glorious: A Biography of General Strong Vincent*. Kearny, New Jersey: Belle Grove Publishing Co., 1997.

Newton, Steven H. *McPherson's Ridge: The First Battle for the High Ground, July 1, 1863*. Cambridge, Massachusetts: DaCapo Press, 2002.

Nichols, Edward J. *Toward Gettysburg: A Biography of General John F. Reynolds*. University Park Pennsylvania: Pennsylvania State University Press, 1958.

O'Neill, Jr. Robert F. *The Cavalry Battles of Aldie, Middleburg and Upperville, Small but Important Riots, June 10–27, 1863*. Lynchburg, Virginia: H.E. Howard Co., 1993.

Peterson, John S and Michael Phipps. *"The Devil's to Pay": General John Buford, USA*. Gettysburg: Farnsworth Military Impressions, 1995.

Pfanz, Harry W. *Gettysburg: The Second Day*. Chapel Hill: University of North Carolina Press, 1987.

_____. *Gettysburg: Culp's Hill and Cemetery Hill*. Chapel Hill: University of North Carolina Press, 1993.

_____. *Gettysburg: The First Day*. Chapel Hill: University of North Carolina Press, 2001.

Priest, John Michael. *"Stand to It and Give Them Hell": Gettysburg as the Soldiers Experienced It from Cemetery Ridge to Little Round Top, July 2, 1863*. El Dorado Hills, California: Savas Beatie, 2014.

Pritzker, Barry *Mathew Brady*. East Bridgewater: JG Press, 1992.

Reardon, Carol. *Pickett's Charge in History and Memory*. Chapel Hill: University of North Carolina Press, 1997.

Redd, Rea Andrew *Altars to Amputations: From Gettysburg Churches to Battlefield Hospitals: A History and Walking Tour*. Savas Beatie, 2020.

Robertson, James I. *General A.P. Hill: The Story of a Confederate Warrior.* New York: Random House, 1987.

Sauers, Richard. A. *Gettysburg Campaign, June 3 - August 1, 1863: A Comprehensive, Selectively Annotated Bibliography*: Greenwood Publishing Group, 1982.

_____. *A Caspian Sea of Ink: The Meade-Sickles Controversy.* Baltimore, Maryland: Butternut and Blue, 1989.

_____. *Meade: Victor of Gettysburg.* Potomac Books, 2004.

Sears, Stephen W. *Gettysburg.* New York: Houghton Mifflin Company, 2003.

Smithsonian Institution. *The Civil War: A Visual History.* New York: DK Publishing, 2011.

Spruill, Mark. *Decisions at Gettysburg: The Nineteen Critical Decisions That Defined the Campaign.* Knoxville, Tennessee: University of Tennessee Press, 2011.

Symonds, Craig L. and William J. Clipson. *Gettysburg: A Battlefield Atlas.* Charleston, SC: The Nautical & Aviation Publishing Company of America, 1992.

Tagg, Larry R. *The Generals at Gettysburg: The Leaders of America's Greatest Battle.* Mason City, Iowa: Savas Publishing Co., 1998.

Trudeau, Noah Andre. *Gettysburg: A Testing of Courage.* New York: Harper Collins Publishers, 2002.

Trulock, Alice Rains. *In the Hands of Providence: Joshua L. Chamberlain and the American Civil War.* The University of North Carolina Press, 1992.

Tucker, Leslie R. *Major General Isaac Ridgeway Trimble: Biography of A Baltimore Confederate.* McFarland, 2005.

Tucker, Philip Thomas. *Storming Little Round Top: The 15th Alabama and Their Fight for the High Ground, July 2, 1863.* Conshohocken, Pennsylvania: Combined Books, 2001.

_____. *Barksdale's Charge: The True High Tide of the Confederacy at Gettysburg, July 2, 1863.* Casemate Publishers, 2013.

Walker, Paula and Robert Girardi. *The Soldiers' General: Major General Gouverneur K. Warren and the Civil War.* Savas Beatie, 2015.

Weigley, Russell F. *A Great Civil War: A Military and Political History, 1861-1865.* Bloomington and Indianapolis: Indiana University Press, 2000.

Wert, Jeffry D. *Cavalryman of the Lost Cause: A Biography of J.E.B. Stuart.* New York: Simon & Schuster, 2008.

_____. *General James Longstreet: The Confederacy's Most Controversial Soldier.* New York: Simon & Schuster, 1993.

Wilson, Clyde Norman. *The Most Promising Young Man of the South: James Johnston Pettigrew and His Men at Gettysburg.* McWhiney Foundation Press, 1998.

Wilson, Robert. *Mathew Brady: Portraits of a Nation.* London: Bloomsbury, 2013.

Wittenberg, Eric J and J. David Petruzzi. *Plenty of Blame to Go Around: Jeb Stuart's Controversial Ride to Gettysburg,* 2nd ed. New York: Savas Beatie LLC, 2006.

_____. *Gettysburg's Forgotten Cavalry Actions.* New York: Savas Beatie LLC, 2011.

Wynstra, Robert J. *The Rashness of the Hour: Politics, Gettysburg, and the Downfall of Confederate Brigadier General Alfred Iverson.* New York: Savas Beatie, 2011.

Made in United States
Troutdale, OR
07/11/2024

21165227R00060